Current and Upcoming Wise Giver's Guides from The Philanthropy Roundtable

Karl Zinsmeister, *series editor*

For all current and future titles, visit PhilanthropyRoundtable.org/guidebook/

TABLE OF CONTENTS

PhilanthropyRoundtable

SERVING
THOSE
WHO SERVED

A Wise Giver's Guide to Assisting Veterans and Military Families

Thomas Meyer

Karl Zinsmeister, series editor

ISBN 978-0-9851265-7-5
LCCN 2013936500

First printing, May 2013
Second printing, August 2013

INTRODUCTION

Fresh, Useful Information for a Young Philanthropic Field

Aid for veterans, military servicemembers, and their families is a comparatively new and very fast-growing branch of American philanthropy. Alas, there is little good information available for donors to help them be wise in their giving. According to the new book *With Charity for All*, fully 60,000 nonprofits have the word "veterans" in their name, and a Defense Department white paper estimates that a total of 400,000 service organizations in one way or another touch veterans or men and women who are still serving. Within this blizzard of choices there are some wonderful and highly productive organizations. There are also lots of feckless and even counterproductive undertakings.

This book will help donors assess the field. It is especially oriented toward helping the latest, post-9/11, generation of veterans. And we make particular efforts to illuminate the places where private funding can act more effectively than government—which pours more than $140 billion into veterans every year, but not very flexibly, and with many gaps. Our main purpose is to help philanthropists make certain their gifts go beyond sentimental support, and actually aid a population that every good American wants to see prosper.

There is much alarmism about veterans today. "Judging from media accounts, I'm the rare American veteran who isn't homeless, homicidal, or suicidal...." started a recent essay in the *Atlantic* by former soldier James Joyner. Much of this gloomy commentary is inaccurate or misleading.

For instance, a definitive government study released in 2013 found that while suicides among veterans rose 10 percent from 1999 to 2010, the suicide rate among the overall population rose much faster during that same period—up 31 percent. And two-thirds of veteran suicides are among those 50 years and older, suggesting the biggest problem is not among men and women deployed since 9/11.

As a group, it is much more accurate to think of veterans as a national asset than as a national problem, or set of victims. Nearly 6 million Americans have served in the military since the 9/11 attacks: 2.8 million of them are still serving; 3.2 million are civilians as of early 2013. Some of those civilian veterans are in college, at home raising children, or retired; of those who are in the labor force, more than 90 percent are employed.

The annual earnings of all U.S. veterans are 12–15 percent higher than the earnings of non-veterans. Their poverty rate is only a little more than half the overall rate.

None of this is surprising when you notice that veterans rank higher than the general population in levels of intelligence, physical fitness, avoiding a criminal record, finishing high school, and attending college. To help you separate realities from the many myths about veterans in circulation today, we have included at the end of this book a set of vital statistics. You'll find clear data on the topics above, as well as others like physical health, mental health, family status, and so forth.

While those who have served in the military are—on the whole—in better shape than comparable non-veterans, there are many individuals who need and deserve help. Foremost among these are the men and women who were injured during their service. In this book, we lay out six areas where there are opportunities for public-spirited donors to aid veterans. In all of these areas, donors and charitable groups are already making progress, though both the successes and the remaining gaps vary a lot by region.

Employment

In 2012's sluggish economy, 9.9 percent of post–9/11 veterans were unemployed. That compared to 7.9 percent of non-veteran workers. Unemployment among vets is elevated among the young; for ages 35 and over, veterans are actually significantly less likely than non-veterans to be unemployed.

This is a great place for philanthropists to concentrate their energies. Corporate donors are particularly able to be helpful. Interestingly, many of the companies doing today's best work with veterans are finding that hiring them can be good for the company as well as for society. Firms like JPMorgan Chase, GE, and Prudential have discovered that locating, certifying, and hiring veterans can actually fill skilled jobs that would otherwise go begging for lack of trained candidates (see cases 2 and 3). One coalition of large manufacturing and high-tech companies plus corporate foundations is driving an effort to help tens of thousands of veterans earn credentials in skilled occupations where there are shortages of workers.

Speaking statistically, veterans are a national asset, not a national problem or set of victims. Nonetheless, there are individuals who need and deserve help.

Philanthropists working to improve the job prospects of people leaving the military are concentrating in three areas: training veterans, placing them in jobs through employment fairs and matching services, and mentoring them so they succeed. See page 160 for examples of some charities and donors active in this field. There is room for much more of this.

Education

One great advantage veterans have today is a G.I. Bill with richer education benefits than ever provided before. Federal money is complemented by matching funds from many private colleges and from private donors. As a result, nearly all veterans can now afford college tuition, occupational training and certification courses, or graduate instruction. Any remaining barriers are less economic than social.

A typical veteran on campus today is 5–10 years older than the common teenage college student. He or she often has a family to support. During summer and semester breaks, going home to live with mom and dad may not be an option. So making the social adjustment to college, getting appropriate mentoring from campus authorities, financing the interstitial periods between semesters, and staying on task until a degree is finished are the toughest hurdles. On page 162 you'll find a summary of some service providers and donors who have discovered ways to be useful in this area.

Physical Health

Some of today's most heartfelt private help for servicemembers and veterans is being offered to nurse the injured back to health. Obviously the primary responsibility for rehabilitating wounded warriors falls on the shoulders of the Departments of Defense and of Veterans Affairs. But savvy philanthropists have discovered many important niches where their interventions can make crucial enhancements in the quality of treatment.

Thankfully, the universe of severely injured individuals is limited. Of the 2.4 million Americans who were deployed to Iraq or Afghanistan, fewer than 15,000 were hurt seriously enough to be evacuated from the theater. The number of persons who have lost a limb is just over 1,700; 4,174 troops suffered penetrating brain injuries; 250 vets are now coping with complete blindness. Because this is not a bottomless pit, it is an area where dedicated charitable effort can have noticeable and lasting effects.

The Fisher family has accomplished miracles in league with allied donors by launching institutions that set new standards of care for amputees, for brain injuries, and for the families of those injured and killed. The Katz Family

Foundation, the Marcus Foundation, and others have placed superb plastic surgery, neurological, and burn services within the reach of wounded warriors. Hundreds of nonprofits are offering injured veterans home modifications, and disabled sporting experiences, and service dogs. Others are training civilian doctors in military culture to help them be effective and sensitive practitioners to veterans. For more examples, see page 164.

Mental Health

Because of the special privacy often desired for mental-health services, private counseling outside the official clinics of the Department of Defense and Department of Veterans Affairs is often valued by veterans and members of the military. Plus, family members, who often are as stressed by overseas deployments and by injuries as the veterans themselves, are in many cases not covered at government clinics. So there are many opportunities for enlightened mental-health services provided by private philanthropy.

One impressive charity has simply organized psychological professionals— ranging from family counselors to social workers to psychiatrists—to donate an appointment or two per week to a veteran on a *pro bono* basis. This has made aid available even in rural areas and towns far from V.A. facilities. Other impressive accomplishments in a range of mental-health services are touched on in cases 8–15.

Family and Community

At any given time, about 2 million spouses and children are sharing family life with full-time members of the military. Because the relatives of servicemembers and veterans often face their own special challenges growing out of the military service of their loved one, various forms of family assistance can be very helpful to them. Veterans themselves often seek community services as well, after they leave the military and begin the transition to civilian life.

On page 168 we list dozens of charities and donors operating in this sector. They range from efforts that support caregivers, to bereavement services. They include groups that enhance the education provided to military children at their schools, and various fraternal organizations offering support, social life, and sporting challenges to vets.

Legal / Financial / Housing

Though veterans are less likely to fall into poverty than other Americans, some inevitably face financial troubles and need help getting back on their feet. Eliminating debt, finding housing, and solving legal problems are all places where philanthropy can help. Case 20 in this book profiles a very savvy charitable effort to bring good financial counseling and crisis management to veterans. Part of their contribution was setting up a system to make sure donors offering emergency funds to veterans in distress were not duplicating each other's efforts or feeding dysfunctional behaviors which would cause problems to recur.

On the legal front, as in mental health, one solution that has been highly effective yet low in cost is donation of *pro bono* hours by professionals. Case 19 details one excellent program that organizes lawyers to help veterans on a *pro bono* basis. Housing is another area where many philanthropic efforts are under way, ranging from special efforts to pluck homeless veterans off the streets and treat their underlying problems, to programs that help veterans become homeowners. On page 170 there's a fuller list of things donors and charities are doing.

Help That Is Practical, Careful, and Hard-headed

This book is intended as a how-to manual for ambitious donors who want to make a noticeable difference. We've sifted through mountains of information so you don't have to, and worked to make this guide practical, concrete, breezily written, packed with interesting case histories, timely and up-to-date, and conversant with many of the most promising people, techniques, and organizations in the field. It is for philanthropists wanting to jump in and help—not casual or theoretical observers.

In addition to being issued in book form, this work will also be distributed as a commercial e-book, and on the Roundtable website. It is the first product of the new veterans program launched by our organization in 2013. We'll be offering more publications, conferences, and aids to military philanthropy in the years ahead. Visit PhilanthropyRoundtable.org for the freshest information on what's available.

We are commencing this new program with a hard-headed focus on actual results. With veterans as in any other charitable effort, good intentions are not enough. In fact, it is possible to do more harm than good when giving away money, if one's vision is not clear. To help our members and other philanthropists walk the fine line between aiding veterans and turning them into dependents robbed of their independence and purpose, you'll find in the very next section of this book a powerful essay about the differences between constructive and destructive aid. It is written by an expert who was himself severely wounded as a soldier in Iraq.

Meanwhile, we hope you will consider joining The Philanthropy Roundtable, entering our network of hundreds of top donors from across the country who debate strategies and share lessons learned. Our meetings are intellectually challenging and entirely solicitation-free. We also offer customized resources and private seminars at no charge for philanthropists who are eager to make the greatest possible difference in their giving.

Please contact us at (202) 822-8333 or main@PhilanthropyRoundtable.org if you would like more information.

The Roundtable is able to offer combinations of assistance to donors without charge thanks to our generous funders. For making the creation of this book and the launch of our new program for veterans and military families possible, we offer our sincere appreciation to five pioneering supporters: The Ahmanson Foundation, the Anschutz Foundation, the Bodman Foundation, the Prudential Foundation, and the Paul E. Singer Foundation.

Adam Meyerson
President, The Philanthropy Roundtable

Karl Zinsmeister
Vice president for publications

Thomas Meyer
Program manager, veterans services

SETTING THE SCENE
Avoiding Perverse Incentives in the Wounded Veteran's Recovery Process

By Daniel M. Gade

A fundamental principle of design in any public-policy program can be found in the ancient Hippocratic Oath: "First, do no harm." This should be especially true of policy toward veterans. Having already taken risks in uniform to protect our society, they should not be exposed to risks from government policy or private philanthropy which could harm them after their service.

Unfortunately, many policies directed toward servicemembers and veterans recovering from wounds of various sorts violate this fundamental rule. While created out of an intention to help the wounded warrior, they often combine to create a perfect storm of disincentives that can cause individuals to become passive dependents during a season of acute distress. Temporary dependency, if improperly managed, can become permanent dependency. Veterans unintentionally robbed of self-sufficiency lose crucial abilities to take part in all that American society has to offer.

Maj. Daniel M. Gade, who holds a Ph.D. in public policy from the University of Georgia, teaches in the Department of Social Sciences at the U.S. Military Academy. He served as a platoon leader and a company commander in Iraq in 2004 and 2005, where he was wounded in action twice and decorated for valor. Despite losing his right leg at the hip, he won his category at Ironman Arizona in 2010, and in 2012 he completed the "Race Across America" cycling race, covering the 3,000 miles from San Diego to Annapolis in eight days as part of a four-man team.

This problem is far-reaching, entrenched, and serious, and I encourage philanthropists and nonprofit organizations to take it into account when designing or participating in programs for helping veterans. Philanthropists should assess opportunities for giving with a gimlet eye: Compassion is no excuse for carelessness. Perverse incentives and moral hazards can corrode veterans as much as anyone else. As with most recipients of aid, the best help is generally that which speeds the beneficiary toward the point where help is no longer needed. Givers who fail to separate fact from fiction, and emotion from reality, may actually create additional burdens for veterans at a vulnerable point in their lives.

How Misconceived "Help" Can Harm

For the sake of argument, let us examine a fictional soldier, Adam,[1] and the forces that affect his reintegration into society.

Adam is from a small town in Kentucky. Although he dropped out of college after his first year, he is the first member of his family to attend college at all. He joined the Army for several reasons: If you ask him, he might say he did it because "they attacked us." Personal desires for life experience, adventure, college money, and structure all played into his decision.

Adam's first tour overseas as an infantry soldier was scary: In Iraq, the insurgency was still very active and dangerous. Although he wasn't wounded, he had a friend killed, and still has occasional nightmares about that day. His second tour, this time in Afghanistan's Nuristan province, was a different story. Four months into his deployment, an improvised explosive device destroyed his Humvee, killing two other soldiers and seriously injuring Adam. He woke up at Walter Reed National Military Medical Center after two weeks of unconsciousness with a mild brain injury, amputation of his lower right leg, and minor shrapnel wounds to his remaining leg, arms, and face.

At first, Adam is just happy to be alive: although he is in some pain, his medical care is excellent and he feels confident that he will recover fully. He has headaches from the mild brain injury, and his shrapnel wounds are taking a while to heal, but his mother and girlfriend are there to nurse him back to health, and he is grateful. He can't wait to learn to walk on his new prosthetic so that he can get back to Kentucky, get out of the Army, and go on with his life.

Adam has an interesting life: the President pinned on his Purple Heart, a Congressman and Senator came by to see him just last week, and the quarter-

---

1. While "Adam" is fictional, neither his medical condition nor his experiences are in any way atypical. His education, background, family history, post-service course, and challenges are all common to veterans who served in the post-9/11 war on terror.

back of his favorite team came by with an autographed jersey. He was invited to join Faith Hill on stage at a concert where 10,000 people gave him a standing ovation. He really likes taking his girlfriend to the festivals, cycling trips, and fancy dinners that are offered to him. As a matter of fact, Adam is beginning to feel like a bit of a celebrity; he may even think, despite the occasional nightmare, that "this rehab gig isn't so bad after all."

After six months, Adam can run again on his new prosthetic leg. A year after his injury, he starts his medical board process so that he can separate from military service, and eight months later he is a civilian. He goes to an advocacy group for disabled veterans for help filing his disability claim, and they insist that he apply for disability based not just on the lower leg amputation (which, in truth, is more of an inconvenience at this point), but also for the shrapnel wounds, mild traumatic brain injury (TBI), and for his bad dreams, which they call post -traumatic stress disorder (PTSD). Fortunately, his claim is handled rather quickly, and the government gives him a disability rating of 40 percent for the leg, an additional 10 percent for the scarring, plus 30 percent for the PTSD.

Compassion is no excuse for carelessness.

He is also offered the chance to go to vocational rehabilitation, or back to college on the greatly expanded new G.I. Bill. On the other hand, his counselor from the Department of Veterans Affairs says that he qualifies for something called "Individual Unemployability." I.U. is a program where someone like Adam, whose disabilities don't add up to 100 percent disabling, can receive compensation at the 100 percent rate as long as he doesn't work. Adam feels like he could work, but the difference between compensation at the 80 percent rate and the 100 percent rate is significant (about $1,000 per month), and he wouldn't have to make all the adjustments involved in going to work every day, so he applies for I.U. and receives it.

Adam is deserving of the praise, support, and love of his fellow Americans. In some ways, it is a natural impulse to give him whatever he needs or desires. Nobody is criticizing Adam, nor do I intend to be the first. In fact, it is useful to compare Adam's case with two other soldiers, also fictional but also based on real people: Bill and Chris.

Bill is a hard-charger, and a member of the U.S. Army Special Forces (a Green Beret). When he was hurt by small-arms fire in Iraq in 2006, his injuries were serious: as a matter of fact, his leg was amputated below the knee like

Adam's. However, Bill has many characteristics that give him advantages over Adam: he is happily married with children, already had completed his bachelor's degree, and, most importantly, has a reservoir of self-reliance and drive that gets him through tough times.

The upshot: Bill not only puts his injury behind him but elects to continue on active duty, and has even returned to combat. Bill, and the many soldiers like him who have stayed on duty in the military or launched successful civilian careers despite serious injuries, will need some helping hands along the way. It is simply not accurate, however, to call Bill "disabled." Nor is he a particularly good target for either government transfer payments or private charity.

Chris, on the other hand, needs all the help he can get. He was a sergeant in the infantry and was serving proudly in Afghanistan when he was hit by an IED and suffered penetrating trauma to his head, leaving him severely disabled. He has crippling headaches, poor mobility, and poor cognition. He is dependent on others for daily activities like cooking, transportation, and many elements of self-care. Chris is a perfect fit for lifelong disability payments and extensive ongoing treatment.

Both Bill and Chris are exceptions. In social science terms, these men are outliers, in the "tails of the distribution." Bill has an exceptionally good outcome, mostly because of internal character traits. Chris has an exceptionally bad outcome, despite his own character strengths. His injuries are simply too devastating. Bill and Chris represent small slices of the total population of wounded, ill, and injured veterans of Iraq and Afghanistan.

Adam, on the other hand, is a much more common case. His situation is thus the one we will examine most closely as a normal baseline to inform the assistance offered to veterans. Both public policy and private charity should be crafted around population norms, not extreme cases (while retaining a degree of flexibility to address those veterans with exceptionally bad outcomes for reasons outside of their control).

Cut Off from Healthy Work and Self-support

It is indeed true that there are many Adams today who end up him permanently and totally "disabled." But *not because of their injuries*. Instead, they are being disabled by well-intentioned charity and governmental support that works as a massive impediment to their reintegration into mainstream society. Let us examine several of these forces.

Financial: Due to his injury, Adam receives $50,000 in Traumatic Servicemen's Group Life Insurance. This money is intended to serve as a bridge to rehabilitation. During his recovery, Adam lives in lodging provided free of charge. He can eat for free at the hospital or other Army dining facilities. He also receives his full salary and other benefits.

Once he leaves the Army, Adam will receive a portion of his military retirement pay and all of his disability benefits from the Department of Veterans Affairs. Because he chose to apply for I.U., he will receive compensation from the V.A. at the 100 percent rate (around $2,800 per month). Depending on where and when he applies, he might qualify for Social Security Disability Insurance[2] as well. SSDI is worth around $800 a month for someone like Adam. All told, his benefits package from the government might be worth in excess of $4,000 per month, most of which is tax-free. Considering that the national median earnings of 20- to 24-year-old males who work full time is $1,908 before taxes,[3] he is doing well. It is in this environment that Adam must make a decision about whether to work or not: because he loses his I.U. benefit and his SSDI if he begins to earn above a minimal amount, he faces a stiff financial penalty for beginning a job. Considering that he has only one year of college, it will initially be difficult to replace that income, much less exceed it.

Psychological: When considering the nature of disability, it is important to consider the difference between diagnosis and impairment. For someone like Adam, his diagnosis was serious at the beginning, but his residual impairment might be mild. So how "disabled" is Adam? From one perspective, he is not disabled at all: He is bright, strong, walks with a slight limp, and only occasionally has headaches or a sleepless night due to his TBI. On the other hand, Adam has just spent more than two years *proving to the federal government* that he is disabled, and not one but two federal programs have labeled him as "disabled." It is relatively easy to imagine that he may begin to label himself disabled as well, with all of the negative psychological outcomes that can bring.

Social: A person's work is a huge portion of how he relates to society, and a key part of his identity. Although each of us has many identities, our work-related identity is typically near the top of the list. Because Adam is labeled disabled by two federal programs, he decides not to get a job. As a result he meets fewer people. In fact, he is pretty isolated at home, and has a much smaller social network than someone who goes to work every day. He is involved in fewer social activities, and more likely to become depressed and experience

---

2. Not all disabled veterans receive SSDI. SSDI is unlike V.A. compensation in that it is "all or nothing." Normally, those on SSDI are seriously disabled. It is entirely possible that Adam would qualify based on his multiple conditions.

3. Bureau of Labor Statistics data for second quarter of 2012.

> People value those things for which they
> strive, and tend to devalue those things that
> are given to them.

other social dysfunction. More fundamentally, he doesn't have the meaning and purpose that comes with work, even when it taxes us.

Charitable: Many charities have been formed in the last decade to assist veterans and wounded warriors, and many existing charities have formed subsidiaries or programs for the same purpose. Someone like Adam might be touched by a half-dozen or more groups providing him things: tickets to events, sporting equipment, cash, dinners, vacations, clothing, a place to live or housing services, and many more. Each one of these types of support is provided with the best of intentions. If there isn't some correlated effort to help Adam enter productive, self-supporting society, however, the downside is that these gifts can cumulatively sap the recipient's willingness to earn those things for himself. It can be difficult for well-meaning donors to accept that this really does happen, but the reality matches the intuition: people value those things for which they strive, and tend to devalue those things that are given to them.

Obviously not every veteran responds to these various incentives in the same way. Some people will take their disability payments and job re-training and make dramatic successes of themselves. Rep. Tammy Duckworth, Wounded Warrior Project board president Dawn Halfaker, Sen. John McCain, and many others have done just that. It's critically important to realize, though, that the men and women who are able to resist the siren song of gifts, charity, and disability payments are often exceptional, and the system should be designed not to harm those who might be lured astray by poorly constructed incentives.

Understanding Disability

The concept of "disability" is a key starting point for helping injured veterans navigate their recovery processes. At least two major models of disability exist, the first of which is the so-called "medical model." The medical model is an attempt to classify a disease or impairment and control its effects. The medical model of disability says that an amputee is "disabled" because of his limb loss.

A more modern approach is the broader "social model of disability," which assumes that a physical ailment is only the first element of disability. The social model adds environmental and personal factors to the physical diagnosis. For example, a wheelchair user has much less mobility impairment in an environment free of wheelchair barriers (curbs, stairs, etc.). Similarly, personal factors at the individual and family level strongly affect the degree of disablement that a person will exhibit at the completion of their medical course of treatment. Many families are able to find "a new normal" after a family member becomes disabled; some are not. Some individuals are resilient in the face of daunting challenges; some crumble.

As a society, the United States has begun to shun the medical model in favor of the social model. The 1990 passage of the Americans with Disabilities Act reduced physical barriers in the built environment and required reasonable accommodation in the workplace. New prosthetic, computer, and drug technologies have had some revolutionary effects. Societal attitudes have changed.

The World Health Organization (WHO) also has adopted a social model of disability in its International Classification of Functioning, Disability, and Health.[4] Most human-resources managers in businesses, government, and non-profit agencies now apply a social model of disability.

We've become accustomed to seeing amputees pass us on the ski hill. Children with disabilities are often put into "mainstream" classrooms. Adults with disabilities are accommodated at many kinds of jobs. Lots of us have watched co-workers find new employment niches with the help of retraining, computerized equipment, or other accommodations. Our views of what is possible and "normal" have been altered dramatically over the last generation.

A key concept for understanding disability today is appreciating that there is a difference between *capacity* and *performance*. Capacity is the best that an individual can be expected to do in a specific area of life. Performance is what that person actually does.

The goal of any program relating to persons with disabilities should be to narrow the capacity-performance gap. In some areas, technology is decisive: A computer that reads materials aloud for a person with dyslexia, for example, may eliminate the gap between capacity and performance entirely. Some prostheses can significantly narrow gaps in mobility, appearance, or performance, if not close them. Alternatively, the gap between capacity and performance may be widened by human behavior. Bullying or negative attitudes toward disability could pull a disabled person's performance far below what he is capable of.

Many government programs acknowledge the social model of disability. For example, most disability employment programs run at the state level require some version of an Individualized Education Plan as part of the re-employment process. These plans take into account the particular strengths and weaknesses

---

4. International Classification of Functioning, Disability, and Health (World Health Organization, 2001).

of the candidate before placing him into a tailored program of rehabilitation, education, or training in independent living.

Writing Checks Versus Re-integrating into Work and Society

Unfortunately, several major U.S. government programs rely on a medical model rather than a social model. The Department of Veterans Affairs disability-compensation program is one. The V.A.'s statutory requirement (found in U.S. Code Title 38) is to compensate for disabilities based on "average loss of earnings" that would be expected in a worker with that particular diagnosis. The V.A.'s compensatory scheme thus relies on two abstractions—a diagnosis, and an estimate of the average loss of earnings of previous persons with that diagnosis. Note that this definition does not take into account personal qualities, or family support, or educational potential, or other factors affecting how much residue of disablement an injury will leave behind.

What this means, in essence, is that the V.A. doesn't base its compensation on disability at all, but rather around a diagnosis. By this definition, those athletes you see sprinting and swimming at the Paralympics, and the wounded veterans now working in many Wall Street banks, are "totally disabled." Some injured servicemembers who remain on active duty and return to what they did before their injuries will, bizarrely, be labeled "totally disabled" once they leave the service. Clearly, the medical model leaves something to be desired.

The Department of Defense has its own separate disability-rating system that superficially resembles the V.A. system. The DoD rates disability based on whether the person in question can still perform his assigned military duties or can be re-assigned to something more in line with his residual capacity. There are dozens of amputees who have returned to service after rehabilitation, and at least one completely blind soldier who continued his Army career after losing sight in 2005. The DoD paradigm is a better example of the "social model." By eliminating barriers and restructuring work requirements, it allows persons with disabilities to continue to contribute usefully to the DoD's work.

The reason that disability systems and supports must be carefully designed is simple: The process of applying and proving that one is "disabled" can trigger a powerful set of social constructs in the disabled person, his family, and his community. Applicants can start to rely routinely on others. Personal aspiration can dry up. Passivity and dependence can become normal.

The modern military is both healthier and more educated than society at large.

The person with a disability may experience a change in "locus of control." Instead of believing that he is responsible for his own outcomes in life (internal locus of control), the person may believe that other people or the environment are responsible for his outcomes (external locus of control). Similarly, the community may begin to view the person with a disability, consciously or not, as an object of pity rather than as a citizen with full standing. Charitable giving which accidentally creates disincentives to work can serve to hasten the onset of displaced locus of control in the person who receives the charity.

In their recent book *The Declining Work and Welfare of People with Disabilities*, economists Richard Burkhauser and Mary Daly study two massive federal programs—Social Security Disability Insurance (SSDI) and Supplemental Security Income (SSI)—and find that despite the last generation's many new legal protections and forms of assistance for the disabled, their employment rates are at an all-time low, support rolls are rising, and household income among persons with disabilities is stagnant. The design of these programs makes work both "less attractive and less profitable" than passively receiving benefits. The positive effects of the Americans with Disabilities Act and other efforts at mainstreaming and integration, the researchers conclude, have thus been considerably nullified by carelessly designed entitlements.

Astonishingly, there are more Americans of working age receiving government disability checks today (more than 12 million) than there are paid workers in our entire manufacturing sector.[5] Through our Social Security system alone, cash payments to individuals classified as disabled totaled $135 billion in the latest fiscal year. It isn't just cold-blooded economists who have noticed this. *New York Times* opinion writer Nicholas Kristof recently acknowledged the problem. "This is painful for a liberal to admit, but conservatives have a point when they suggest that America's safety net can sometimes entangle people in a soul-crushing dependency."[6]

The disability system for veterans is bedeviled with this problem. Benefits are predicated on an individual first proving a work-related disability or handicap, causing individuals to become economically and emotionally invested in their condition as a barrier. And the primary focus is on cash assistance, rather than on helping the individual get rehabilitated, retrained, and reoriented so he can

---

5. Nicholas Eberstadt, "Trim the Entitlement Machine with Disability Reform," *Think Tanked*, December 5, 2012, http://www.washingtonpost.com/blogs/thinktanked/wp/2012/12/05/fiscal-cliff-do-democrats-have-a-plan-for-cutting-entitlements/

6. Nicholas Kristof, "Profiting from a Child's Illiteracy," *New York Times*, December 7, 2012.

engage in productive labor. The many psychological, social, and financial benefits of work are thus often lost to recipients.

Because systems giving cash to the disabled are filled with perverse incentives, Burkhauser and Daly suggest enhancing employment and offering other mainstreaming services, instead of just writing checks. They offer a series of reforms using the Dutch model of rewarding and thus incentivizing work. While their recommendations adhere to the particular nature of the SSI and SSDI programs they are writing about, the parallels between the deteriorating trends they review and the veterans disability system are striking. Despite improved technology, deepened legal protections, and greater acceptance in public opinion, V.A. disability enrollment has exploded, the number of different medical conditions claimed by recipients has mushroomed, and the official rates of functional impairment among V.A. clients have essentially remained stagnant over the last several decades.

> Despite the many assets of today's young veterans, there are reasons for serious concern in current dependency trends.

The unfortunate incentives identified by Burkhauser and Daly may actually be worse for wounded warriors than for private-sector workers. Not only does the individual face the moral hazard of being tempted to substitute a cash entitlement for daily labor, but there is also a greater moral hazard for the employer. The Department of Defense bears no burden when an employee exits the military with a disability settlement, since the V.A. handles the caseload, and taxpayers pay the tab. The normal risks of simply cutting checks rather than undertaking the work of rehabilitation and integration are thus actually worsened by the nature of public employment.

A New Generation of Veterans

The post-9/11 generation of veterans has borne heavy burdens accumulated during more than a decade of war. Deployments have been unusually long and unusually frequent. Fortunately this generation of servicemembers has many strengths and assets that have helped them meet these demands.

First, the modern military is composed solely of volunteers. And rather than being a random cross-section of society they are, as a statistical fact, both healthier and more educated than society at large. (See "Vital Statistics" at the end of this book.) With very few exceptions, they are high-school graduates or have GEDs, and many even in the enlisted ranks have college experience. More than 80 percent of officers have bachelor's degrees, and many have graduate degrees. Most of the veterans of Iraq and Afghanistan are young—still in their 20s—and because our current military's medical and physical fitness standards are relatively rigorous, veterans are both physically and mentally healthier than the population at large. A final demographic difference is that the Afghan and Iraq wars involved record levels of Reserve and National Guard forces, who are typically somewhat older, even more educated than the active force, and more fully integrated into civilian life in other ways.

Second, the combat experience of today's veterans is markedly different than most previous counterparts. With a few exceptions (the initial invasion of Iraq, the first and second battles of Fallujah, isolated pockets of the fighting in Afghanistan, and a few other episodes), today's veterans have faced conflicts characterized by chronic, low levels of violence rather than dramatic, high-intensity battles. At the same time, they have largely operated in theaters with no front lines and with civilians mixed in with combatants. This means they have often been exposed to civilian suffering and also been unsure of their adversaries.

> Well-intentioned programs often create side-effects that are not at all what the program's creator desired.

Third, the social and economic environment experienced by veterans after their service is much different today than for some previous generations. By and large, the civilian world is now accepting of its veterans and thankful for their service. In some circles this is called the "Sea of Goodwill"[7] and encompasses not just grateful citizens, but employers, community leaders, government officials at all levels, academics, health care professionals, and others. There are hundreds of major charitable programs and thousands or tens of thousands of minor programs and donors who have stepped up to provide a welcoming environment for returning soldiers and recently discharged veterans.

Finally, although the number of veterans to be re-integrated is high, it is still dramatically less than in previous wars. Fewer than 2.5 million veterans have served in Iraq or Afghanistan since 9/11.[8] That is less than served in

---

7. This phrase was coined by Adm. Mike Mullen in a 2008 Memorial Day speech, and is the title of a DoD white paper, "The Sea of Goodwill: Matching the Donor to the Need."

8. DoD reports that 2,443,927 individuals had been deployed to Iraq or Afghanistan as of June 30, 2012.

Vietnam, and only a fraction of the 16 million Americans who served in the military during World War II.

The upshot of all of this is that, contrary to some conventional wisdom, it is a serious mistake to look at veterans overall as victims, or as a problem class. Both the earnings and the overall income of veterans in this country are higher than those of non-veterans. Among all males, for instance, year-round workers averaged $51,230 in 2009 if they were veterans, and $45,811 if they were non-veterans.[9] The advantage for veterans is even bigger among women. And when the measure is "income" (including not just earnings but also pensions and entitlements), veterans fare even better.[10]

Given their educational and health advantages outlined above, Iraq and Afghanistan veterans are likely to be a valuable asset to America's economy and society over the coming decades. It is not all veterans who need help, but just particular veterans working through transitions to civilian life, or struggling with specific personal burdens, who may need assistance from fellow citizens.

Dramatic Increases in Compensation

Despite the many assets of today's young veterans, there are reasons for serious concern in current trends. A staggering 45 percent of Iraq and Afghanistan veterans are currently seeking compensation for service-connected disabilities.[11] They are applying at more than twice the rate of troops who served in the 1990s Gulf War. Currently, about a third of all new veterans are being granted some level of disability. And the number of disabling medical conditions claimed by the average applicant has soared from 1 or 2 among post-World War II veterans, and 3 to 4 among Vietnam veterans, to 8.5 medical conditions per claimant among veterans who served in Iraq and Afghanistan.[12]

Those are shocking numbers. They are influenced, however, by many inducements in today's system, including V.A. procedures. The definition of

---

"Deployment File for Operations Enduring Freedom, Iraqi Freedom and New Dawn" (Contingency Tracking System Deployment File Baseline Report, Defense Manpower Data Center, 2012).

9. Because this figure does not take into account the selection effects of the high initial enlistment standards, this difference would be slightly less if we compared people who served with those who could have served but chose not to. Nevertheless, this simple figure illustrates that veterans are doing quite well on average.

10. U.S. Department of Veterans Affairs, *Profile of Veterans: 2009*, http://www.va.gov/vetdata/docs/SpecialReports/Profile_of_Veterans_2009_FINAL.pdf

11. For a brief layman's summary of Department of Veterans Affairs data, see http://news.yahoo.com/ap-impact-almost-half-vets-seek-disability-16065648lhtml. For a more thorough academic treatment, see http://costsofwar.org/sites/default/files/articles/52/attachments/Bilmes Veterans Costs.pdf.

12. Statement of Department of Veterans Affairs Under Secretary for Benefits Allison Hickey before the House Committee on Oversight and Government Reform, July 18, 2012, http://oversight.house.gov/wp-content/uploads/2012/07/7-18-12-Hickey-Testimony.pdf

disability in the V.A. system is such that most of these veterans are not "disabled" in the commonly used sense of the term. More accurate terminology would describe them as "having a service-connected condition."

The most prevalent service-connected condition in the V.A. system in 2011 was tinnitus (ringing in the ears), and the second-most prevalent was hearing loss. Of the nearly half-million post-9/11 veterans receiving disability compensation in 2011, 16 percent were granted 10 percent disability, 38 percent were given 20–40 percent disability, 42 percent were paid for 50–90 percent disability, and 4 percent were compensated for 100 percent disablement.[13]

Some small part of the jump in medical conditions per claimant may be explained by the happy fact that some servicemembers whose injuries would have killed them in previous wars are now saved by improved trauma care. But that is a minor factor. Keep in mind that out of the 2.7 million servicemembers who have served in Iraq or Afghanistan, less than 14,000 were wounded in action seriously enough to merit evacuation from the theater.

> The old saying about giving a man *a* fish versus teaching him *to* fish applies in veterans philanthropy as much as anywhere else.

It is appropriate for the nation to spend whatever it takes to help seriously injured servicemembers recover their capacities. Thankfully, catastrophic injuries are less common among post-9/11 veterans than generally imagined. For example, there are about 1,700 amputees. Approximately 250 Iraq-Afghanistan veterans are blind. About a hundred suffered spinal-cord injuries. And penetrating brain injuries total 4,174.

PTSD is the affliction most mentioned in popular discussions. It is a syndrome covering a very wide range of complaints, and estimating its prevalence is complicated by the fact that there have been at least two major policy changes in PTSD diagnosis and treatment. First, the V.A. no longer requires proof that a traumatic incident occurred. (Indeed some advocates argue that there need not be any precipitating incident, that PTSD can occur simply from an accumulation of occupational pressure.) Second, the V.A. actively seeks patients instead of just accepting them when they come. This latter deci-

---

13. *V.A. Annual Benefits Report*, 2011, http://www.vba.va.gov/REPORTS/abr/2011_abr.pdf, accessed September 23, 2012.

sion gets more veterans into treatment, but also makes the total number much higher. Among Iraq and Afghanistan veterans, the Department of Veterans Affairs reported 217,082 cases of diagnosed PTSD as of the first quarter of the 2012 fiscal year, a significant increase in prevalence compared to previous generations of combat veterans.[14]

The Department of Veterans Affairs is also loosening rules for qualifying for benefits on the basis of traumatic brain injury. In December of 2012 the agency unveiled new regulations that will make it easier for thousands of veterans to receive benefits for five additional diseases, basing the expansion on a 2008 Institute of Medicine study which found "limited or suggestive" evidence that these diseases may sometimes be linked to TBI.[15] Incidentally, only a small fraction of the 250,000 cases of TBI diagnosed among servicemembers since 2000 are combat related. The vast majority stem from vehicle crashes, training accidents, or sports injuries.[16]

Categories of Assistance and Their Pitfalls

A returning service member or recent veteran in need may benefit from assistance in areas like medical care (physical and/or psychological), education or training, or employment. Obviously much depends on circumstances—whether the service member is headed for redeployment by his unit, repatriation to civilian life, or rehabilitation from a significant trauma.

A rich network of services would first treat acute and chronic medical needs, then provide rehabilitation services as needed, and finally help veterans gain and maintain useful employment, all roughly in that sequence. At each stage, the needs of the soldier or veteran can be met by federal programs, by assistance from state or local government, by nonprofit groups of various stripes, or by individuals—family members, neighbors, church congregants, or donors.

When services are being offered to individuals, dangers can arise in the area of perverse incentives or unintended consequences. This is a well-known phenomenon in economics—well-intentioned policies or programs often create side-effects that are not at all what the program's creator desired, but which can be as pronounced as (or even stronger than) the intended good

14. Office of Public Health, VHA, Department of Veterans Affairs, "Analysis of V.A. Health Care Utilization among Operation Enduring Freedom, Operating Iraqi Freedom, and Operation New Dawn," March 2012.

15. Institute of Medicine, *Gulf War and Health: Volume 7, Long-term Consequences of Traumatic Brain Injury*, http://www.iom.edu/Reports/2008/Gulf-War-and-Health-Volume-7-Long-term-Consequences-of-Traumatic-Brain-Injury.aspx

16. "Rules Eased for Veterans' Brain Injury Benefits," *New York Times*, December 7, 2012, http://www.nytimes.com/2012/12/07/us/benefit-rules-eased-for-veterans-with-brain-injuries.html?_r=0

result.[17] It is a truism of public policy that "if you want more of something, subsidize it." If the thing being subsidized carries downside risks, recipients may be hurt as well as helped.

This trend is visible in the stark growth of disability programs of all types over the last several decades. After reviewing the 19-fold explosion of disability claimants since 1960, *Washington Post* columnist George Will warns that "gaming . . . of disability entitlements" has made work "neither a duty nor a necessity"—which is one major reason why the male labor force participation has plummeted from 89 percent in 1948 to 73 percent today.[18] Federal agencies like the Government Accountability Office have called repeatedly for serious reform of incentives in disability programs,[19] warning that "low return-to-work rates may be due, in part, to the timing in which certain supports are offered to beneficiaries."[20]

Programs for veterans are no exception to this problem. Compensating individuals for their disabilities will result in more people lining up to be declared disabled,[21] just as unemployment programs invariably increase the time that people in receipt of compensation remain jobless.[22] It makes policy-makers and taxpayers queasy to think that programs designed for good can be crippling to intended beneficiaries if incentives are misaligned. But it's clear that poorly designed compensation programs can serve as a "headwind" that holds back veterans from long-term success, rather than an aid.

This isn't just a risk with government entitlements. Some charitable programs designed to honor veterans can also have negative effects. One troubling trend in charitable giving has been the growth of programs offering large gifts to veterans based on service-connected disability. For example, there are several programs offering free homes to veterans who have been declared disabled. Such programs, while heart-warming in the short run, may serve as a chilly headwind in the long run if they decrease a veteran's desire to participate in the labor force. It isn't particularly hard to balance out the negative incentives in such generous gifts—via sweat-equity requirements like those

---

17. For example, a recent *New York Times* article discussed how the global carbon-credits market had the effect of causing factories in China and India to overproduce a certain polluting chemical so that they could sell the carbon credits earned when its byproducts were destroyed.

18. He notes that the number of workers receiving disability compensation rather than working has jumped from 455,000 in 1960 to 8.6 million today. George Will, "Mugging our Descendants," *Washington Post*, October 26, 2012.

19. For an excellent summary of this ongoing problem, see GAO Report 03-119, January 2003.

20. GAO Report 08-635, May 2008.

21. For a taste of this research, see David Autor, Mark Duggan, and David Lyle, "The Effect of Transfer Income on Labor Force Participation and Enrollment in Federal Benefits Programs: Evidence from V.A.'s Disability Compensation Program," Massachusetts Institute of Technology, 2010.

22. See for instance "Job Search and Unemployment Insurance: New Evidence from Time Use Data," by Alan Krueger and Andreas Mueller, *Journal of Public Economics*, April 2010.

> Poorly designed assistance for veterans—governmental or charitable—can actually hurt and disable the intended beneficiary.

used by Habitat for Humanity, financial co-pays, and concrete expectations of employment after the recipient moves in—but those important details are currently lacking in most programs, at least in part because the charities that do this type of work generally haven't developed the will and capability to provide the required oversight.[23]

Principles for Doing Good without Doing Harm

Neither today's federal programs for veterans nor the thicket of charitable offerings to the same population are in any way intended to harm veterans. Yet it is quite possible for them to drag down recipients during their transition from service to civilian life. How, then, can donors and charities interested in caring for veterans provide crucial support without creating disincentives to full recovery and reintegration? Here are some helpful principles:

1. **Always take incentives into account, including negative ones.** Veterans are simply people, and they respond as rationally as they can to the incentives they are offered. The old saying about giving a man *a* fish versus teaching him *to* fish applies in veterans philanthropy as much as anywhere else. Does the program that you are considering creating or donating to *provide for veterans,* or does it *help them integrate into society and assist them in providing for themselves*? Paradoxically, a program that offers benefits to a veteran only as he enters work might be better for him than one that subsidizes him in his unemployment, even though the unemployed veteran is more miserable.

2. **View veterans as resources, not damaged goods.** The percentage of veterans who leave the service totally and permanently

---

23. The Repair Corps program run jointly by the Home Depot Foundation and Habitat for Humanity has thought through some of this. It provides improvements to the homes of disabled veterans—not only wheelchair ramps and widened doorways, but also roofing, electrical, plumbing, insulation, and structural repairs. A combination of volunteer labor from Home Depot employees (trained by Habitat volunteers), plus $2.7 million of funding from the Home Depot Foundation recently allowed the program to expand. But the repairs are not a gift. Participating families agree to repay a zero-interest loan to cover the costs of the remodeling, and the repayments are put into a revolving fund to assist other families.

disabled is tiny. The percentage who need or could use some help is moderate. The majority of veterans need no special help at all. Efforts to help veterans should start by appreciating and valuing all that they can bring to an employer or community, and should focus on moving veterans from the category of needing some help to the category of self-sufficiency. Offering them independence is the biggest favor one can do.

3. **Don't reinvent the wheel.** Some existing charities and rehabilitation efforts are excellent and can serve as a model for further efforts. If your contributions are large enough to change the ways that programs operate, then reinforce the ones that create healthy incentives for self-reliance, and push other well-intended programs away from negative incentives they may have unintentionally created. Insist on these things as a condition of your support.

4. **Every human success is a victory.** It is not necessary to change the lives of all veterans for the better. If you try, you will likely frustrate yourself with failure. Instead, focus on concrete, attainable goals, and *change even a few lives for the better.*

The warnings we've posted here—that poorly designed assistance for veterans, governmental and charitable alike, can actually hurt and disable the intended beneficiary—are rarely spoken, partly because they can so easily be attacked for demagogic purposes. But these are hard realities, ones I have observed both through years of academic specialization in this area and through personal experience. I was wounded twice in Iraq. The second time I nearly lost my life, did lose my entire right leg, and ultimately required more than 40 operations before I could return to self-supporting work and family life.

During my year at the Walter Reed medical center, I saw many, many soldiers who had been moderately wounded, like Adam, get sidetracked from their reentry into productive society by overly generous or poorly targeted programs. One soldier, a below-knee amputee from the 2nd Infantry division, used his traumatic injury settlement of $100,000 to buy not one but two new luxury cars. That money could have changed his life for the better had it been devoted to job training, a starter fund for a small business, or the purchase of a home.

I myself was offered forms of help along the way that could have sidetracked my quest to regain independence. I was also blessed by wiser offers from generous helpers at hundreds of points along the way, and by a supportive and loving family. But far too many veterans are disabled by poorly designed incentives and programs before they even get out of the starting gate.

I want to emphasize that the cautionary spelled out in this text is only half the story. The other part of the tale is that the vast predominance of charitable assistance offered to veterans today does wonderful things, for men and women who deserve support. And most of the individuals who have served our country in uniform will respond well to wise incentives, and end up as highly productive civilians.

But as you read this book, and feel inspired to create or expand a philanthropy for veterans, servicemembers, or their families (which I certainly hope you will consider), do so in smart and hard-headed ways. The flip side of avoiding bad incentives is the imperative to offer smart incentives. Donors who do so can dramatically increase the opportunities for today's veterans to participate fully in the American dream without headwinds or handicaps.

OPPORTUNITIES FOR PHILANTHROPY

So: you have a passion to improve the lives of those who have served their country in the American military. What can you do that will have a significant impact? The choice will obviously depend on the areas you feel most strongly about (physical healing? jobs? education? family life?). It will depend upon your time frame, your specific objectives, your tolerance for risk versus certainty, and of course your budget.

The Philanthropy Roundtable quizzed experts in the field and collected ideas about where a donor may be able to achieve good things—either in a new area, or by building on existing work. You will find a range of possibilities below. Remember, these are general concepts, not implementation plans.

Employment

This is a wide-open field, where the services provided by the government to demobilizing servicemembers are not very good, where companies are already doing some interesting work, and where the real action is on the local level. Despite today's elevated unemployment rates, many companies are finding it hard to locate enough skilled workers in fields like computer programming, welding, nursing, electrical contracting, machining, mechanical and electronic repair, and so forth—areas where many vets have training and experience. Bridging the skills gap in alliance with local employers and educators is a natural fit for community philanthropy. Every part of our country has particular job needs with specific employers, so there is no single path.

- Gather your local and regional business leaders from different industries to determine the feasibility of creating local training pathways and job pipelines for veterans. Donors might offer to match contributions made by firms supporting these training programs at local community colleges. Learn from the examples already pioneered by groups like GE, the Manufacturing Institute, Futures Inc., Prudential, and Workforce Opportunity Services (see case 2).

- Fund a program to train veterans in entrepreneurship and small business ownership. The Entrepreneurship Bootcamp for Veterans with Disabilities run through Syracuse University, and the Kauffman Foundation's FastTrac Veterans Initiative are two existing examples, but given the comparatively small numbers they are able to educate each year there is room for other programs in the same mold.

- Fund a career-mentorship program that connects successful professionals with young military veterans. American Corporate Partners has already begun some work in this area that you could build upon.

- Lead efforts to reduce the government regulatory barriers (mostly at the state-government level) that prevent well-trained military specialists from being certified in equivalent civilian occupations. There should be fast tracks that allow combat-medics to be quickly certified as EMTs and military truck drivers or computer programmers to earn equivalent civilian licenses without undue hurdles.

- A more general problem philanthropists might work on: a generation ago, only 5 percent of U.S. jobs required occupational licenses; today 30 percent do. Is it fair and sensible for states to demand licenses, fees, and training ordeals before individuals take up work as fitness instructors, barbers, mechanics, tax preparers, cooks, taxi drivers, security guards, landscapers, etc.? Many of these are fields into which military-trained individuals could slip seamlessly, except where licensing requirements are an obstacle.

- Help one of the existing job-matching programs, like Hiring Our Heroes, operated by the U.S. Chamber of Commerce, bring an employment fair for veterans to your area.

Education

The biggest issue in higher education as a whole today is not getting students into college but getting them to graduate. Almost half of all students who begin college at a four- or two-year institution currently fail to complete their studies within six or three years, respectively. That wastes resources, needlessly elevates personal and federal student debt, and leaves the dropouts without a degree or credential that has value to them and to society. With veterans perhaps even more than other students this is the issue to focus on. Keeping them enrolled and helping them succeed so they graduate on time requires a combination of cultural training for college administrators, financial gap-filling, and mentoring services. Another way to improve the family welfare of veterans and servicemembers is to help spouses (who don't enjoy as much tuition assistance) attain higher education.

- Fund studies at your local colleges on how many veterans drop out while using their G.I. Bill benefits, and why. Compare completion rates for different institutions, programs, and student backgrounds.
- Fund your alma mater to join the Yellow Ribbon Program—which provides financial assistance covering the difference between G.I. Bill contributions and actual college costs at expensive private institutions.
- Fund programs that bring small cohorts of military veterans onto campuses all at the same time, while providing advance training and mutual group support in order to make sure the college experience is successful. Programs like the Posse Foundation and Year Up are just beginning to do this on a small scale, and there is much room for expansion.
- Fund colleges to run their own pre-semester orientation programs specifically to welcome veterans to campus and help them succeed once there. Many colleges already do this for inner-city students, minorities, foreign students, etc., so similar efforts for veterans could be created quickly and easily.
- Start a revolving or no-interest loan fund to help student veterans make ends meet if their G.I. Bill funding gets delayed (as often happens in the V.A. bureaucracy). A small bridge loan that allows the student to start the semester and then gets repaid within a few months can make the difference between dropping out and not.
- Fund summer stipends to support summer internships for veterans attending college or university on the G.I. Bill (which does not support students between semesters).

- Look for other adaptations that can help colleges welcome veterans, support them once they are on campus, and prevent them from dropping out, recognizing that veterans can be very different from traditional students.
- Support the higher education of spouses of servicemembers and veterans. That's a back-door way of bolstering the household income and well-being of military households.

Physical and Mental Health

The Departments of Defense and Veterans Affairs spend tens of billions of dollars on health care and counseling. Sometimes philanthropy can be most helpful just by aiding individuals in navigating the bureaucracies to find services. But inventive donors and charities have also found many niches where they can directly provide care that is enthusiastically welcomed by servicemembers and veterans. Sometimes this involves filling geographic gaps, other times private services are cherished for the greater privacy they allow, or the extra quality or specialty coverages that focused philanthropy can provide. Support for family members who are the main caregivers for most wounded warriors is an area where philanthropy has been tremendously helpful.

- Fund high-end care in medical specialties that military hospitals are not always well equipped to offer—like plastic and reconstructive surgery, specialized neurological recovery, stem-cell therapies, and so forth.
- Fund facilities that integrate a wide range of medical care on V.A. or DoD medical campuses. For example, the Intrepid Fallen Heroes Fund has begun building six satellite centers for the treatment of brain injuries and traumatic stress. The Lilly Endowment funded the Richard Roudebush V.A. Medical Center to open a seamless integrated care clinic.
- Advocate with elected officials and the Departments of Defense and Veterans Affairs for changes to our current disability system to put more emphasis on aggressive rehabilitation up front, so that injured servicemembers can take up productive careers, and less emphasis on long-term benefit payments that treat injured individuals as permanent dependents on the government.
- Remind policymakers that new technology, legal protections, and social views now make it possible for many of the disabled to become independent, yet government programs encourage them to collect checks rather than work. Even among soldiers who have had one limb amputated, fully 20 percent return to active military duty rather than retiring to civilian life, and as many as 5 percent have actually been returning to combat. Modern accommodations make it possible for most wounded veterans to live satisfying, dignified, and self-supporting lives; our military disability

systems need to be turned on their heads to emphasize intensive rehabil-itation and help make independence easier, rather than just pensioning off the injured with long-term reparations.

- Fund continuing education for civilian medical professionals (in both physical and behavioral health) to aid their work with military pop-ulations. Encourage them to join the military's Tricare health-provider network. Purdue's Military Family Research Institute has already worked on this throughout the state of Indiana; Give an Hour is working to train the next generation of mental-health providers nationwide.

- Consider convening mental-health providers in your area to share best practices for treating veterans, along the lines of the McCormick Foun-dation work described in case 14.

- Fund colleges to include veterans and the military in curricula used to train social-service professions. Both CUNY's Silberman School of Social Work and USC's School of Social Work have begun offering coursework on these topics.

- Fund tele-health networks so that veterans who live in places with no close providers, or family members who don't qualify for counseling, can still consult medical and behavioral specialists. Give an Hour (case 12) has organized professional counselors willing to donate their services *pro bono*; helping Give an Hour deepen its network in your locality may be an option.

- Fund a civilian hospital that treats servicemembers, veterans, and their families to incorporate mental-health screening and treatment into its primary care. Scott & White Hospital near Fort Hood, Texas, has created a good model (case 13).

- Fund scientific evaluations on whether service dogs help mitigate trau-matic stress symptoms.

- Fund scientific evaluations on how effective participation in various "adaptive sports" is in helping injured veterans recover.

- Fund scientific, anonymous, evaluations on how effective the *pro bono* ser-vices offered by Give an Hour are in helping veterans heal. If significant benefits can be documented, there is great potential for even wider donation of *pro bono* professional services from a range of medical disciplines.

Military Families

As mentioned above in the context of employment, sometimes the best way to assist a service member or veteran is to make life easier for his or her family. That might mean getting a spouse a job or education, or enhancing the education offered to children of military families, or just enhancing the quality of life of households that must cope with a great deal of mobility and occasional spikes of profound stress.

- Help military spouses succeed in jobs and careers that can move when the household is relocated. That can elevate both income and satisfaction levels in military families. Donors might fund fellowships for training or accreditation in mobile careers like realty, tax preparation, teaching, financial counseling, nursing, a whole range of online jobs, etc. The FINRA Foundation, for instance, has sponsored more than 1,200 military spouses to earn Accredited Financial Counselor certificates.

- Fund schools that serve significant numbers of military children to implement the same high-caliber curriculum and teacher preparation as their peers in other states have. The National Math and Science Initiative has already spread this to roughly one-third of military-affected schools in the country (see case 17).

- Fund research on the number and characteristics of family members providing care to wounded veterans at home; examine their needs and whether there is assistance that could make them more effective and comfortable. The Elizabeth Dole Foundation has begun some of this work already.

- Fund research into the needs, attitudes, and challenges of military families. Blue Star Families conducts an independent annual survey of military families.

- Consider funding a quality-of-life initiative for military families, which may emerge from surveys of obstacles they are facing in coping with deployments or other strains.

Legal and Financial

This is another area where there are opportunities for expanded pro bono *services from supportive professionals. They can provide very-high-quality services for a very modest price, sometimes with donors funding the administrative office or matching service or other charitable infrastructure that links vets in need to professionals willing to help. Legal help and services like financial counseling may sound prosaic, but solving problems in those areas can eliminate or reduce a whole cascade of secondary pressures. Financial counseling, for instance, can head off unsustainable behavior before it reaches a crisis point. Prophylactic philanthropy of that sort is both humane and efficient, because interventions are made before the household is in meltdown.*

- Fund a veterans clinic at a local law school, legal aid organization, or network of *pro bono* lawyers to provide legal services. Models exist at John Marshall Law School, William & Mary School of Law, and the Connecticut Veterans Legal Center and its Yale University clinic (case 19). "When philanthropically financed lawyers take cases, or intelligently match cases with *pro bono* lawyers, and work with local law-school clinics, they're leveraging a lot of resources for a fairly small budget," notes Mike Wishnie of Yale Law School.

- Replicate veterans treatment courts in your local community, or propose legislation making other pre-trial diversionary programs accessible to veterans throughout the state. New York State Health Foundation has supported replication of veterans treatment courts in the past; and the Connecticut Veterans Legal Center helped enact a law in Connecticut that opened courtroom alternatives to vets. See pages 138–143 for ideas.
- Fund a central clearinghouse to assess and administer emergency financial assistance for veterans and servicemembers. This can save time and trouble for both donors and recipients, and reduce bad funding decisions. VeteransPlus has built one model (case 20).
- Fund financial-counseling organizations to counsel recipients of financial aid and make sure they don't fall back into the same financial problems that caused distress initially.

Housing and Homelessness

Some very active philanthropies run by groups like Home Depot and Habitat for Humanity, as well as lots of local variants, have done a pretty good job of helping wounded veterans adapt (or find) houses that don't interfere with their medical condition. This is life-changing work, but luckily there are not large numbers of seriously wounded individuals who require adaptive housing. There is federal and state assistance available to help veterans buy houses and to rescue those who have fallen into homelessness. But sometimes the nimbleness of private giving is important in bridging time delays and filling cracks that large bureaucratic programs often develop.

- Fund security deposits, utility down payments, and furnishings for homeless veterans moving into transitional housing. Government housing vouchers for homeless veterans (HUD-VASH) do not cover deposits and furnishings, which can significantly delay housing placements for veterans and encourage chronic homelessness. "Unmet needs like these can extend the time it takes to move a homeless veteran into an apartment by weeks or even months," says Tom Nurmi, of Funders Together to End Homelessness. The William S. Abell and Conrad N. Hilton foundations have been first-movers in providing philanthropic support to complement and enhance government grantmaking in this realm.
- Set up repayable revolving funds to help disabled veterans upgrade their housing beyond what V.A. grants may cover.

Other

Sometimes the mechanisms used to provide assistance matter as much as the size or the content of the aid. Some philanthropists are currently experimenting with community-wide consortia that try to provide more of a "one-stop-shopping" experience for veterans. Others, rather than reinventing the wheel, are asking their charitable partners to consider adding veterans to existing groups they offer social services to. Especially creative donors might consider bringing advanced philanthropic approaches to veterans work—by establishing new donor-advised funds focused on serving this population, for instance, or by experimenting with social-impact bonds.

- Fund a call-in generalized referral service for veterans, servicemembers, and their families at some local organization. The San Antonio Area Foundation funded the United Way to bring veteran specialists into its 211 referral service; in New York, the Robin Hood Foundation has funded Iraq and Afghanistan Veterans of America to open a call center to help connect veterans in need to Robin Hood grantees who provide direct services.

- See if there is a need in your community for a one-stop-services hub along the lines of what Swords to Plowshares has provided to veterans in the San Francisco area for nearly 40 years (case 1).

- In all of your funding, require grantees to begin tracking whether their clients have ever served in the military. Adjust services as necessary with this information.

- Consider setting up a national donor-advised fund dedicated specifically to helping veterans, servicemembers, or their families, so that other individuals, foundations, and corporations can work together on philanthropic causes.

- Commission a feasibility study to determine if social-impact bonds might be appropriate for solving issues facing veterans. So-called "Pay for Success" bonds are contracts under which investors use private capital to provide services that improve social outcomes. If the results are more effective or cost less than what government has been providing, then investors receive as a dividend a portion of the savings realized by the government. An organization called Social Impact has studied the feasibility of using such private problem-solving incentives in other populations. Among veterans, there might be opportunities for dramatically new approaches to disability compensation. Instead of writing a lifetime of small checks to the disabled, perhaps social impact bonds might be used to front-load an intense array of services to re-train wounded warriors, so that they could increase their earnings potential and self-sufficiency, rather than relying on transfer payments for the rest of their days.

CASE STUDIES

The great philanthropist Julius Rosenwald used to say it was harder to give away a million dollars well than it was to earn that much money in the first place. If you are serious about really helping people with the money you donate, one of the best places to start is by studying what successful givers have done before you. Seeing how others have navigated the field which interests you can provide both instruction and inspiration of the highest order.

At business schools, the leading techniques of commerce are taught via case studies. Seeing the details of how one firm triumphed is thought to be the best way to help the next generation of entrepreneurs find successes of their own. From great business to good charity: What follows are 20 cases outlining some of the very best philanthropy that has been accomplished over the last decade or so on behalf of veterans and servicemembers. There are examples here from the full range of topics covered in this guide: jobs, schooling, physical and mental health, family life, and so forth—all boiled down to their highly readable essentials.

Spending an hour or so reviewing these highlights from excellent recent giving may be the single best way for donors to make themselves great military philanthropists in the future.

PHYSICAL HEALTH,
MENTAL HEALTH,
FAMILY LIFE, JOBS,
HOUSING

Priming the Pump:
David Gelbaum gives
big, and early

In 2006, David Gelbaum, an entrepreneur and former investment analyst, opened a then-anonymous
donor-advised fund with the California Community
Foundation. He said it would be dedicated to supporting the needs of military servicemembers and their
families. Gelbaum placed $105 million in the fund, and
later committed another $138 million to the cause.

Gelbaum's donation became the largest single philanthropic gift benefiting those serving in the military after the 9/11 attacks. What he called the Iraq-Afghanistan Deployment Impact Fund (IADIF) was so large that it required special staffing. The California Community Foundation asked Nancy Berglass, a consultant with nearly three decades of experience in grantmaking, to become director of the fund during the limited time when it would be pushing money out the door.

$243 million is a lot of money to give away. It seems even bigger when it has to be committed in three years, and still larger when the field in which it has to be invested is largely new and undeveloped. Reflecting on the fund's origins, Berglass says:

> Originally I had some concern about taking this on. I questioned how effective I could be attending to the donor's intent when I did not at the time have expertise in his area of interest. I quickly learned, though, that there was no history of organized philanthropic intervention on behalf of veterans and the military, and no known set of standards or best practices for serving this population through nonprofit organizations. So there was this tremendous leadership opportunity before all of us.

Although military philanthropy was a relatively blank slate, the donor's intent was not—within one year he wanted the initial $105 million committed to organizations providing direct services. While obviously veterans organizations did exist, very few organizations were set up to serve the specific needs of those serving in the current wars. "It was a challenge to identify best-in-class organizations so early in the trajectory of this generation of servicemembers."

Moreover, "there was neither a strong familiarity with military culture amongst grantmakers, nor any reliable data available to give us a fair assessment of the scope of service-related needs of post-9/11 veterans," noted Berglass. "Any assumptions we made would have been based on personal feelings, which are not enough to inform smart grantmaking." So Berglass enlisted experts to fill gaps in existing knowledge.

Researchers at the RAND Corporation were hired to provide an overview of the issues affecting veterans, servicemembers, and their families, and the existing service providers. Based on this initial guidance, the IADIF identified broad areas on which to focus. These ranged from medical needs to housing and financial assistance, from employment help to aid for children and families.

Picking the Right Organizations

While this research helped identify broad needs and gaps, it provided no checklist for vetting organizations worth funding. (Even with several more years of research and experience since then, there still is no simple way of identifying worthwhile grantees. That is why The Philanthropy Roundtable has created this book and launched a veterans philanthropy program to sharpen future work.)

While some exciting philanthropy resembles venture-capital work—finding diamonds in the rough and providing them with capital to grow—a lot of effective philanthropy goes to support proven organizations. Berglass and colleagues directed Gelbaum's money to a wide variety of grantees—ranging from big, established veterans groups, to startups created to address emerging needs of those who served in Iraq and Afghanistan, to civilian nonprofits opening new programs to serve the military community.

For example, $43 million in grants from IADIF went to philanthropic projects launched by the Fisher family (whose work is profiled in case 8). The bluest of blue-chip philanthropies supporting the military and veterans, the Fisher House Foundation and the Intrepid Fallen Heroes Fund have had decades of success in this area, and were ideally positioned to quickly turn grants into high-impact projects benefitting the wounded. The IADIF joined with the Fisher family on three major projects:

- It supported the construction of eight new Fisher Houses—home-like, no-cost housing for family members caring for injured servicemembers as they recover at medical centers.
- It led funding of the Center for the Intrepid, a groundbreaking rehabilitation center for amputees and burn victims in San Antonio.
- It was a major supporter of the National Intrepid Center of Excellence, which researches, diagnoses, and treats traumatic stress and brain injuries.

The vast majority of IADIF's 54 grantees, however, were either new organizations or new entrants to this field. Most mixed strengths and weaknesses.

David Gelbaum's $243 million donation became the largest single philanthropic gift benefiting those serving in the military after the 9/11 attacks.

The new organizations focused on those who served in Iraq and Afghanistan and were often staffed by veterans themselves, but lacked organizational sophistication. More general-service organizations often had solid infrastructure, but were unproven in reaching the populations desired.

Gelbaum initially stipulated that his support go directly to client services. In his second and third rounds of funding, however, some of his money was dedicated to building up the managerial prowess of grantees. This left them in stronger positions to deliver results with future funding from IADIF or other donors.

Tragedy Assistance Program for Survivors (TAPS), a group that provides emotional support to the survivors of deceased servicemembers, is an example of this latter type of funding. While the organization had already been in existence for more than a dozen years, $6.6 million in support from IADIF catalyzed explosive growth for the organization. The group reorganized itself and recruited and trained an expanded corps of volunteers. That allowed TAPS to serve more than 35,000 grieving family members, friends, and casualty officers by the end of 2012.

"Grantmakers have to be mindful that when they invest in smaller, emerging, or grassroots organizations, their investments are more likely to show returns if they help the organizations mature," suggests Berglass. Other groups that benefited early in their formation from IADIF's mix of direct-service and organization-building grants include Operation Mend (profiled in case 9), Operation Homefront, and Homes for our Troops.

There were also a number of examples where IADIF funded successful existing organizations to make their first forays into military-related assistance. The creators of *Sesame Street* were given $6.75 million to create a series of educational TV programs aimed at helping military children adjust to parental deployment and return, and sometimes loss. The initial RAND research had shown that "there were very few resources assessing and addressing the needs of military children," says Berglass, "particularly those of National Guard and Reserve servicemembers, who were deployed more than ever before but who often lived far from the services that active-duty families utilize at military bases." About 400,000 copies of the television episodes and accompanying parent guides were eventually distributed to military families.

Tapping a Rooted Success

Founded in 1974 and operating in the San Francisco Bay area, Swords to Plowshares is one of the country's leading local organizations devoted to providing practical help to veterans. It provides health, housing, job, legal, and social services to more than 2,000 vets every year. IADIF gave the group $5.1 million in a series of targeted grants to zero in on those who served in Iraq and Afghanistan, then help other organizations learn the particularities of serving that new cohort.

Back in 2005, Swords leaders had a sense that the wars in Iraq and Afghanistan were going to produce significant numbers of veterans. With $75,000 in grants from the Walter and Elise Haas Fund, the Richard and Rhoda Goldman Fund, and the San Francisco Foundation, they tried to get ahead of the curve and understand how they could best address the issues facing today's servicemembers.

Younger veterans, they discovered, did not want charity and were hesitant to identify as homeless or in need of help. Swords hired a coordinator to visit armories, post-deployment events, schools, churches, V.A. facilities, and other places where they might find veterans. To get people in the door, Swords focused on its employment programs. Today, around 10 to 20 percent of its clients are post-9/11 veterans.

During its intake process, Swords determines what problems may complicate the veteran's successful reintegration. "It's very rare that somebody comes to us for a job and everything else in their life is just fine," says Amy Fairweather, who directed the initiative for younger vets. "They might have health issues, housing needs, three months of unpaid utility bills, or family trouble. Problems don't happen in a vacuum."

While many veterans organizations focus on one problem and refer clients to other organizations for different issues, Swords provides a broad complement of services in-house. Its endgame is to help veterans live independently. For most persons, Swords provides intensive services for a short, but critical, period of time.

Fairweather describes one veteran who came in homeless and caught up in the justice system, but, with some short-term transitional housing and counseling, was able to turn his life around. "He now has a master's degree in social work from Columbia University. He's working, he's paying taxes, he's happily married, and he's helping his fellow vets."

In addition to trying to make its longstanding programs more accessible to younger vets, Swords has also started new programs to serve the particular needs of those who have served during the last decade or so. In response to the growing number of female veterans, for instance, the organization recently secured a $1 million grant from the California Wellness Foundation to support female veterans. It will be re-granted to 20 organizations statewide.

Having been funded for decades by donors like by IADIF, JPMorgan Chase, Walmart, Prudential, Tipping Point Community, and the Charles and Helen Schwab Foundation, Swords to Plowshares knows the value of diversifying its funding streams. "Funders are all different—some want to be involved, some are hands-off," says Fairweather. In some cases, Swords will seek guidance from funders. Other times, in the case of IADIF for example, Swords plays the role of expert, providing technical assistance to donors and grantees. Fairweather sees private and government funding as complementary. "Government funding is great, but it can be very rigid. Private grant funding allows us to be more responsive on the ground."

Cultivating Expert Partners

Particularly in its first years, when David Gelbaum's desire to provide immediate help was most urgent, IADIF "simply didn't have the bandwidth or the local intelligence to make direct-service grants in all of the American communities hit hardest by deployments," according to Berglass. So Gelbaum and Berglass devised a strategy for sending a portion of the money to community foundations around the country, relying on them to re-grant funds to the best recipients in their area, using their local knowledge of effective charities and potential beneficiaries.

With Texas and Florida hosting large military populations with high deployment rates, IADIF provided $45 million to community foundations in each of those states. These foundations had the freedom to make grants to address the most pressing deployment-related needs in their regions. (The story of one of these re-grants is told in case 13—describing Dallas Foundation support for mental-health counseling near Fort Hood.)

Deeper research eventually became another priority. When IADIF first contacted RAND in 2006 for a quick assessment of the needs of veterans, servicemembers, and their families, the research organization listed several areas where future, more detailed, investigation might fill important gaps in knowledge. At the time, the fund had no intention of funding research. They were an action entity.

Yet "one of the issues we kept running up against with our grantees was that they did not have access to data needed to inform their programs," says Berglass. "This was particularly true in the realm of mental health." Recognizing that addressing some pressing issues would require more information, Berglass encouraged Gelbaum to approve some research.

RAND eventually received $3.5 million from IADIF to inquire in three areas: "What is the nature and scope of post-deployment mental-health problems among returning Iraq-Afghanistan servicemembers? What are the consequences and costs associated with those conditions? What do we need to do to address them?"

In April 2008, RAND released *The Invisible Wounds of War*. It became something of a landmark study on traumatic stress and brain injuries. With over 375 academic citations, 600 media references, and 50 citations in Capitol Hill testimony or legislation, it is an example of how research sponsored by private philanthropy can influence understanding of an issue.

EMPLOYMENT, EDUCATION

Military to Manufacturing
GE and other companies funnel vets to skilled jobs

"It was March of 2012 when our chairman, Jeff Immelt, said, 'We need to look into this,'" recalls Rebecca Edwards, director of employee communications at GE. The intersection of elevated unemployment among veterans with the difficulty many manufacturers were experiencing in finding skilled workers was the topic Immelt wanted his team to investigate. Soon Edwards was investigating ways of turning technically trained veterans into needed employees, with the charge of finding "a solution that made sense for us—that wasn't just charity: that was going to contribute to our goals."

Unemployed veterans were one problem—a national social issue in need of response, from the company's perspective. Another problem that more directly affected GE's corporate interests was 600,000 unfilled jobs across America in high-tech manufacturing. Fully 82 percent of manufacturers now say they are unable to find adequate employees for all of their skilled production jobs. Over the next decade, it is projected that America will have 2.6 million jobs for which there will be a shortage of workers with the necessary skills.

"Veterans were a solution," says Edwards. "We need to train a skilled work-force if we're going to take advantage of future economic trends. It's not just a charity effort."

This attempt to address two concerns at once laid the foundation for GE's Get Skills to Work Initiative. Instead of separating the social problem (unemployed veterans) from the economic problem (lack of skilled labor), GE saw these as different aspects of one big kink in the talent pipeline. There are obstacles preventing high-quality workers from flowing into an American manufacturing industry that needs them.

"I'm an economist. My expertise is workforce economics—connecting supply and demand. We're constantly tracking and mapping the high-demand careers at a state and regional basis," explains Geoff Cramer, the CEO of Futures Inc., originally a nonprofit growing out of the Fuqua School of Business at Duke University and now a philanthropically-minded private company. "Today's top-50 high-demand careers represent 1.7 million job openings and $136 billion in gross annual wages. Baby boomers are aging out of the workforce at a rate of 10,000 per day, and we are on the front end of the greatest talent shortage in American history. We can't even keep up with the replacement rate for many skilled jobs right now, let alone projected growth."

There is a silver lining for veterans in that skills gap. Cramer reports that, "in those top 50 career fields, the largest single pool that matches the skill sets of our highest-paying occupations is military personnel." Yet unemployment among veterans today stands somewhat above that of non-veterans. (See details in the employment figures within this book's statistical appendix.) So where is the disconnect?

The fact is, many veterans are waltzing right into good civilian jobs after they leave the service. Their technical training and work disciplines serve them well, including at manufacturing firms like GE. But a significant minority of veterans find it tricky to translate their military experience into something that will be valued by civilian employers.

In 2012, half of all the expenditures on unemployment compensation for ex-servicemembers went to individuals from just 11 specific military occupational specialties. (There are more than 8,000 military occupational specialties in total.) If credentialing and retraining efforts are properly focused, there are a number of ways to help veterans jump over the moat separating military work from manufacturing, retail, and service-sector work. And success in those endeavors will help veterans, American companies, and the larger U.S. economy alike.

Good Work, Good Works, and Good Business

The ultimate goal of the Get Skills to Work Initiative is to connect veterans with serious jobs where they can apply and build on technical skills they learned while in the military. Linking veterans to workplaces where they will be appreciated and relied upon is one of the most basic things any party can do to help vets flourish in civilian life. Finding good work for former members of the military can thus be categorized as a philanthropic cause. But it is also good business.

> GE's initiative addressed two problems at once: Helping veterans, and pulling skilled workers into a manufacturing sector that desperately needs them.

As one of the country's largest heavy manufacturers, GE needs employees who can run machines, calibrate instruments, and work in teams to build complicated devices. And when the company resolved to help rebuild the talent pipeline between workers and high-skill manufacturing plants, it didn't do so based purely on its own hiring needs. "We have an ecosystem of suppliers around us so we can manufacture the big things we do. Our growth is dependent on our supply chain being able to grow. So we wanted to make sure we were serving their talent needs as well. There's an interdependency," says Edwards. To support this ecosystem, the Get Skills to Work Coalition translates military experience into civilian qualifications, accelerates training in high-demand industries, provides opportunities for veterans to explore careers in high-tech manufacturing, and helps employers retain military talent.

GE began at its aviation business in Cincinnati, Ohio, where the company already had a well-established training program for skilled workers at

Cincinnati State Technical and Community College. The company invited other corporations in the area—including Alcoa, Lockheed Martin, and Boeing—to join it and its nearly 30 regional suppliers. The group quickly drew up a list of what skills would likely be needed in Cincinnati in the near future.

The Manufacturing Institute, a nonprofit organization dedicated to improving and expanding manufacturing in the United States, was brought in to help transfer military experience to civilian certification, and to establish the training paths needed between community colleges and manufacturers short on skilled workers. LinkedIn and Futures Inc. were added to serve as platforms where employers could post jobs and obtain matches with military talent. The Institute for Veterans and Military Families (described in case 3) was included to help employers recruit veterans. This was particularly important for smaller manufacturers, who "don't have giant human resources departments like ours," notes GE's Edwards.

Matching Military and Civilian Skills

As often as possible, the Get Skills to Work Initiative aspires to transition veterans directly into open manufacturing jobs without heavy retraining. Unfortunately, translation of military technical skills into certified civilian occupations is often an obstacle, because each state has different certifications and licenses, all of which are different from those the military uses.

Many employment programs for veterans focus on finding the right words to communicate military experience to civilian employers on a résumé. The Manufacturing Institute's partnership with Futures Inc. aimed to do more than that. They created direct skills-based translations between military and civilian training and experience, and then set up a system to distribute these skill "badges" to veterans over online platforms like Futures and LinkedIn that match talent with jobs.

"It becomes part of your digital portfolio that you carry around with you forever," says Brent Weil of the Manufacturing Institute. The institute had already been working on creating universal, accepted skill badges for some time when GE contacted it to help with veterans. "We got a grant from the University of California Humanities and Research Institute to build digital badges for manufacturing skills—initially we were doing that for youth programs like Project Lead the Way, and Skills USA," explains Weil. In 2011, the Manufacturing Institute won a grant from the V.A. to develop digital badging for transitioning military experience into a civilian career in manufacturing. That was the starting point that GE picked up on.

"The idea behind the badge is that it becomes verifiable, and that it becomes searchable, clickable," says Weil. "We have worked with Futures on a digital platform called U.S. Manufacturing Pipeline where veterans and manufacturing companies and educators can meet up and make job matches." Although funded by a corporation for business purposes, the badging effort serves the philanthropic purpose of helping qualified veterans get good positions with manufacturers in need of their skill sets, and improving the efficiency of the overall labor market.

Making It Easier and Cheaper to Get Supplemental Training

Not all transitioning servicemembers, however, possess the exact skills they need to enter the civilian workforce directly. Just as with digital badges, the Manufacturing Institute had already been working on ways of improving worker training by the time GE approached the group for help with veterans. Closing "the gap between today's high unemployment and the huge number of positions in manufacturing that are open because they require a certain set of skills" has been the focus of the Manufacturing Institute for much of the last decade, according to Weil.

Educational institutions tend to focus on producing highly specialized workers, like engineers, through intensive training programs. But these programs require large upfront investments of time and resources. Meanwhile there is a need for simpler, quicker, less traditional certifications that can make large numbers of workers valuable in the workforce. Weil explains:

> The skills most in need are not things that are hard to attain. Many are in "middle skills" positions, requiring instruction but not necessarily a four- or even two-year degree. Machinists, welders, production workers. Applied mathematics, the ability to follow instructions, safety procedures, quality control, basic production skills—these are the things needed.

The vast majority of these mid-level skills, once acquired, are transferable between positions and companies. For the Manufacturing Institute, the answer is simple—ramp up the production of workers with certifications in these mid-level skills for which open jobs exist, by accelerating training programs.

In 2011, the institute committed to credentialing 500,000 workers by 2016. And persons trained by the military are right in the mix. Working with the Department of Defense along with the Manufacturing Skills Standards Council, American Welding Society, National Institute for Metalworking

> For today's 50 highest-demand careers, military veterans are the largest single pool with the required skill sets.

Skills, and Society of Manufacturing Engineers, the institute folded civilian manufacturing certifications right into existing military technical training. That way, when veterans come out of the service, they already have the necessary civilian credential.

GE also asked the Manufacturing Institute to set up an accelerated training program for veterans who required additional schooling beyond their military skills. GE funded the institute to develop a curriculum that would be validated across manufacturing as a whole, and to work with local community colleges to build the pathways to employment that would fill the needs of GE, its manufacturing partners, regional economies, and veterans. The Manufacturing Institute had already established eight- and 16-week models for some specialties like welding, so it built on these.

The pilot program specifically for veterans launched in January 2013 at Cincinnati State, with 45 students. The plan is to train up to 200 veterans before the year is out to work in GE's aviation plant in Cincinnati. The wider Get Skills to Work Coalition aims to certify 100,000 veterans in needed skills, and place 15,000 of them immediately in jobs. It has 10 new pilot cities where the work is being led by manufacturing giants like Lockheed Martin, Boeing, and Alcoa.

GE's efforts to link veterans to manufacturing jobs illustrate the value of partnership in some complex forms of philanthropy. Realizing that it did not have the expertise to translate military skills to civilian certifications, or to convince community colleges to develop specialized training programs, the company used creative philanthropic donations to nonprofit groups to fill those gaps. And by adapting existing programs to serve veterans rather than building new ones from scratch, GE was able to be effective quickly. Veterans looking for good jobs right now can be grateful for those good practical decisions.

While GE's work with the Manufacturing Institute does not constitute philanthropy in the traditional sense, it is an investment that solves social ills and produces benefits that extend far beyond the confines of the company's own bottom line.

Training Veterans to Order for Skilled Jobs

Workforce Opportunity Services (WOS) is a nonprofit founded by Columbia University business professor Art Langer to help students from low-income neighborhoods step into skilled jobs that companies like Prudential, Merck, Johnson & Johnson, Sealed Air Corporation, and United Rentals are having trouble filling. Here's how it works: companies sitions to part-time work at the company paying the contract. Next there is a full-time trial period, after which point the company decides whether to hire the candidate permanently. During the training and trial period, participants receive compensation for their work at the company, health insurance, credits that easily transfer to local commu-

> Prudential asked Workforce Opportunity Services to adapt its proven model to train veterans for positions at the firm. Other corporate partners soon followed.

contract with WOS to provide a certain number of candidates with a very specific skill set for a particular job—computer programmer, account manager, whatever. WOS then builds a curriculum for the job, contracts with a local educational institution to teach it, and recruits and screens candidates to join a training group of around a dozen people.

The program begins with full-time education, but slowly tran-

nity colleges, and mentoring support from WOS to help them transition to corporate life.

The arrangement is a win for everyone involved. The participants get an opportunity to earn college credit and a stipend while learning marketable skills. Companies are able to fill high-skill positions without having to go into the in-house training business. The program is very expensive—it can cost around

$40,000 per individual—but the largest portion of that goes as pay to the individuals working part-time for the company, for which the company recoups some direct value. Moreover, in-house training can also be very expensive, and is often less successful. It is estimated that most companies earn back the money they spend on WOS candidates in an average of 13 months.

In 2005, Prudential became the first corporate partner of Workforce Opportunity Services. Several years later, Langer reports, Prudential CEO John Strangfeld was speaking to a military officer at his alma mater, the University of Virginia, who asked him, "Sir, thank you for your support of military officers in business school, but are you doing anything for the soldiers we led?" The question spurred Strangfeld to action. Prudential began searching for a program to specifically help enlisted veterans find meaningful, career-oriented employment after their service.

By this point, the company had already seen WOS succeed with high-school students. They thought, why not modify the program to serve veterans? With a few changes that recognized veterans' unique circumstances and contributions— years of experience and maturity, families to care for, and potential service-connected challenges—WOS trained its first group of veterans in 2010, again for Prudential. Other corporate partners soon followed. Currently, Workforce Opportunity Services has 129 veterans working at client companies while they complete their training, and has completely transitioned 27 of its first group of veterans to full-time employment in corporate jobs.

3

Mixing Business and Philanthropy, Improving Both
JPMorgan Chase puts veterans to work

In mid-2010, JPMorgan Chase (JPMC) was just another large American bank with a substantial but fairly traditional corporate philanthropy program, and no specific focus on serving veterans, servicemembers, or their families. Two years later, it was racking up an impressive list of philanthropic accomplishments on behalf of veterans. The company itself and its charitable foundation had led its corporate peers to commit to hiring 100,000 veterans over 10 years, co-founded the nation's leading center for research on employment and educational outcomes among veterans and military families, committed to giving away 1,000 mortgage-free homes to veterans in serious need, and funded a free technology-certificate program for returning veterans. JPMC's work in this area is impressive not only for its size and programmatic creativity, but also for the way in which its business and philanthropic arms mutually support one another.

A Quick Recovery from a Mistake

In late 2010, the U.S. Department of Justice sued JPMorgan Chase and three other banks for violating the Servicemembers Civil Relief Act (SCRA), a law which suspends civil actions against deployed servicemembers until they return from war. JPMC had inadvertently begun foreclosure proceedings on 18 homes belonging to deployed servicemembers, and failed to lower interest rates properly on several thousand others. "We are sorry and regret the mistakes," said Frank Bisignano, the head of Chase Mortgage Banking. "We hold ourselves accountable . . . and we want to move forward from this experience to be an outstanding partner to the military across all of our businesses."

In addition to repaying all of the overcharged members of the military, and in many cases granting the foreclosed homes back to their tenants mortgage-free, JPMC decided to begin actively investing in servicemembers in a big way. The company focused its efforts on education, employment, and home ownership—places where its position as a major American employer with a mortgage business and an interest in recruiting well-educated talent would allow immediate action.

The company promised to award 1,000 mortgage-free homes to veterans and military families within five years. They developed a connection to the Military Warrior Support Foundation (MWSF), a group that offers mortgage-free houses to severely wounded veterans. When the foundation locates a needy wounded veteran, or the spouse of one killed in action, it approaches its bank partners about donating, from their stock of foreclosed homes, an appropriate house in the desired area.

This process requires three forms of careful sifting: finding the right families; matching them with the right home; and providing the right follow-up support services. JPMC could handle the logistics of transferring houses, but had no expertise in assessing recipients or providing services to ensure that the families succeeded in their transition to homeownership. So to make good on its 1,000-house pledge, the company sought out charitable partners: not only the MWSF but also Building Homes for Heroes, Operation Homefront, Homes for Our Troops, and Dallas Neighborhood Homes.

The award programs run by these charities have safeguards to ensure the donations result in a successful transition to home ownership. Recipients must have been honorably discharged from the military, they must use the awarded home as their residence, they must not have an existing mortgage, and they are precluded from taking out a second mortgage on the home or immediately selling it. The veterans and their families must be responsible for insurance, upkeep, and all other costs associated with owning a home. These safeguards were put into place to protect both the integrity of the program and the new homeowners. By erecting clear guardrails around the program, potentially serious failures are headed off.

In addition to sorting and selecting the veterans who would benefit most from these homes, the nonprofit partners are responsible for providing follow-up support services to ensure long-term success. Each program is different in its details, but most offer counseling on budgeting, regular phone check-ins and visits, and help when special needs arise. JPMC's charitable foundation complements the real-estate contributions of its mortgage division by making cash grants to support its nonprofit partners in carrying out these duties. In two years, Chase provided 430 homes to charities serving veterans, and the company has no plans to stop soon.

When Philanthropy Is Good Business

The area where JPMC has arguably had its largest effect on the well-being of veterans and their families is where its philanthropy is closely matched to its own business interests. The firm aggressively recruits, hires, and works to retain veterans. It also funds educational efforts that make veterans desirable employees. JPMC pays for training programs that lead to technology certificates, funds an acclaimed program that provides entrepreneurial education, and convenes its corporate peers to encourage the hiring of veterans.

Some of this work blurs the lines between smart business and effective philanthropy. It certainly improves the employment prospects of veterans and military families. It has also brought a talented pool of employees into the company.

In 2007, JPMC had partnered with Syracuse University to launch a training and certification program called Global Enterprise Technology (GET) which prepares graduates to operate corporate computer systems.

Four years later, as JPMC considered how to expand its commitments to veterans, broadening the GET program was an obvious first step. The resulting Veterans Technology Program is a new online course, administered free of charge, that yields four technology certificates that are valued by employers (and thus valuable to those who earn them).

Just as JPMC's initial relationship with MWSF eventually begot a 1,000-home award program, so did the GET collaboration with Syracuse University eventually lead to a much larger investment there in veteran employment and education. Syracuse has a history as a veteran-friendly institution, and when JPMC was casting about for constructive ways to boost former servicemembers, bank executives met with Syracuse chancellor Nancy Cantor; James Schmeling, the director of the university's well-regarded center for educating the disabled; and business professor Mike Haynie.

> JPMorgan Chase founded the nation's leading center for research on employment and educational outcomes among veterans, with a $7.5 million grant.

Haynie, himself an Air Force veteran, is a professor of entrepreneurship (a specialty of S.U.'s Whitman School of Management), and in 2007 founded one of the most successful programs ever created for wounded vets. The Entrepreneurship Bootcamp for Veterans with Disabilities is an intensive course that provides disabled veterans with the skills necessary to start their own businesses. It has so far trained more than 700 veterans—free of charge, thanks to its generous philanthropic supporters—with a majority of the graduates founding new companies. (See pages 62–64)

Haynie now proposed that the university and JPMC consider forming an institute focused on real actionable research—about education, employment, and wellness for servicemembers transitioning back into the civilian economy, and their families. Soon, thanks to a $7.5 million five-year grant from JPMC, the Institute for Veterans and Military Families (IVMF) was born at Syracuse University under the leadership of Haynie and Schmeling. IVMF fills three primary roles: It conducts scholarly research on issues facing veterans. It runs educational and vocational programming for these populations, such as the Entrepreneurship Bootcamp for Veterans with Disabilities, and the Veterans Technology Program. And the organization helps employers and schools recruit, retain, and serve vets and their families.

Many of the institute's components already existed, Schmeling explains, but were simply not organized to help veterans specifically. "We work with the best academics wherever their subject matter overlaps with veterans. Most of them are experts in other disciplines, whether disability, or national security, or business ownership."

Supporting Academic Research to Advance Practical Outcomes

In addition to its philanthropic effects, JPMC's investment in IVMF has yielded organizational and human-resource returns that ultimately improve the company's bottom line. IVMF has become a source of technical expertise for many employers who are interested in recruiting, training, and retaining veterans as productive employees. Many of them say the program has not only helped veterans but also been valuable to companies looking to fill positions with reliable and skilled workers.

> JPMorgan Chase led 11 large companies in pledging to hire 100,000 veterans by 2020. Within less than two years, 99 companies had joined the coalition.

IVMF releases a variety of practical products on a regular basis. These include monthly veteran-employment reports; weekly briefs that summarize the practical implications of academic research on topics relevant to veterans; and the *Guide to Leading Policies, Practices & Resources: Supporting the Employment of Veterans & Military Families*—the current standard for best practices, culled from research with more than 30 of the nation's leading employers of veterans.

In addition to putting its own cash on the barrelhead, JPMC uses its status as a major American company to convene audiences for the institute's findings on veteran education and employment. In March of 2011, JPMC led 11 large companies in creating the "100,000 Jobs Mission"—a pledge to collectively hire that many veterans by the year 2020. Through January 2013, 99 companies had joined the coalition and collectively hired 51,835 veterans.

Hiring and training 100,000 new workers, of any background, is no easy task. The firms that sign the pledge participate in quarterly meetings where successes and disappointments are shared. This is another place where IVMF has proven a valuable facilitator. The institute has someone at nearly all of the coalition meetings and participating in its calls. IVMF staff serve as subject-matter experts on what various companies are doing and what strategies seem to be succeeding.

"It is one of the best opportunities we have to engage with employers around the country," explains Schmeling. "We brief our latest research topics to them, offer areas where we can be of assistance, and share our Veterans Technology Program in case they want their veterans to go through that. What we get back is the ability to learn from the employer experience—what issues they're facing, how they're dealing with them, where they have challenges they don't yet know how to resolve."

The collected effect of all this is a distinct enhancement of employment opportunities for veterans. "Because those companies know they have a resource who can help them when they need it, I think they become more likely to make veteran-hiring commitments. They're willing to look at veterans whom they otherwise perceive as harder to hire—because we have expertise in disability accommodations, in employing National Guard and Reserve members. They can rely on us," Schmeling explains.

IVMF also smooths collaborations between private firms that, under other circumstances, act as competitors. For example, IVMF is currently working on a means of aggregating human-resources data from different companies. The proprietary nature of the information would normally prevent companies from sharing it, but IVMF has the ability to aggregate and analyze the numbers, then release them so many firms can learn from them, while protecting the privacy of each contributing company.

That kind of collaboration is good for veterans. It is also good for the corporations making the business efforts and philanthropic donations. This is an instance where business and philanthropy productively operate hand in hand.

Entrepreneurship Bootcamp for Veterans with Disabilities (EBV)

In 2006, after serving in the military for 14 years, Mike Haynie left his position as an instructor at the Air Force Academy to take a position as a professor of entrepreneurship at Syracuse University's Whitman School of Management. As he reflected on his own transition from military officer to college professor, "I thought teaching at a civilian university would be very much like what I had just been doing for the past couple years. Honestly, it wasn't. It took me a while to wrap my head around what the heck I had just done leaving the military. In retrospect, I think I was looking for a way to stay connected to the only thing I had known for the previous decade and a half."

That same year, Haynie began advising a student writing a dissertation about entrepreneurship among immigrants. While reviewing general literature in this area, he learned that people with disabilities (who, like immigrants, often have difficulty procuring traditional employment) pursue self-employment and business ownership at a rate twice as high as those without disability.

"As I'm thinking about that, I'm also reading reports," he says, about seriously wounded soldiers "transitioning from military to civilian life." Haynie describes these severely injured vets as "a good news/bad news story." The good news is that, because of advances in battlefield medical care, servicemembers today survive wounds that would have killed them in previous wars. The bad news is that those individuals may have to deal with sometimes-severe disability for the rest of their lives.

This was Haynie's "aha!" moment. "Here I am, a vet, an entrepreneurship professor at one of the top entrepreneurship programs in the United States. Why can't we take something we already do very well—which is teach and train people to be business owners—and refocus that expertise to create a social venture that provides those kinds of resources to transitioning servicemembers with disabilities?"

He brought the idea to the dean of the Whitman School of Management, a Vietnam veteran himself, and received immediate institutional support. Haynie had to find funding to pay for it, as he refuses to charge disabled veterans for any part of the program. And of course he had to invent the curriculum, structure the classes, and recruit participants.

Individual donors like Martin Whitman, Richard Haydon, Steve Barnes, and Ted Lachowicz played key roles in getting the program off the ground. (See "Expanding Entrepreneurship" in the Spring 2011 issue of *Philanthropy* magazine.) One philanthropist, a highly successful entrepreneur, helped Haynie think through the difference between a traditional academic program and the vocational program with practical guidance that EBV aimed to be. He asked, "What are the elements we need on day-one of launching a business in order for the start-up to resonate?"

Another important funder helped Haynie navigate the world of philanthropy, suggesting that he establish a separate EBV Foundation, the sole purpose of which would be to accept funding for the program, rather than simply funneling all of the grants through Syracuse University. "It was an insight I never would have had on my own. I was too new to philanthropy at the time," says Haynie. "And, as a matter of fact, Walmart doesn't like writing checks to universities, and when our relation-

ship was brand new, being able to have them donate to EBV Foundation saved that deal." Walmart later gave $1 million to the program.

Just six months after the idea had been proposed, the Entrepreneurship Bootcamp for Veterans with Disabilities hosted its first enrollees. Since that initial class at Syracuse, EBV has trained more than 700 would-be entrepreneurs—and a remarkable 57 percent have already gone on to start businesses, for which they hired 670 employees. The program's dramatic successes quickly brought requests to duplicate it on other campuses. EBV has now expanded to seven partner universities around the country.

Realizing that the audience for entrepreneurship training goes beyond just disabled veterans, Haynie created Entrepreneurship Bootcamp for Veterans' Families (EBV-F), and Veteran Women Igniting the Spirit of Entrepreneurship (V-WISE). The successes of these programs have led the U.S. Department of Defense to ask Haynie and the EBV team to develop

> Just six months after the idea had been proposed, the Entrepreneurship Bootcamp for Veterans hosted its first enrollees. Since then, more than 700 would-be entrepreneurs have been trained, thanks to generous donors.

an entrepreneurship track within the Transition Assistance Program that the department offers to all servicemembers leaving the military.

Like a lot of successful programs, there were points early on where the entire effort could have collapsed. "We almost didn't have a first class," admits Haynie. "We had massive interest, but when it came time for people to actually follow through, we weren't converting them to applications."

One mistake EBV made was trying to recruit at V.A. facilities. Veterans proved skeptical of the V.A., and the V.A. was skeptical of outside programs offering services in their orbit. "It totally backfired," says Haynie. "It took us the better part of a year to recover from that." While EBV has since come to work closely with both the V.A. and Department of Defense, EBV's best recruiting tool has turned out to be program graduates themselves. "Every time we offer a class, the challenge of filling the next one becomes easier and easier and easier."

The EBV program itself breaks down into three phases. During the first phase, which lasts several months, students work through a self-directed online curriculum from home to develop a business plan. In phase two, EBV brings students to one of the eight EBV campuses to participate in an intensive nine-day

residency program with 24 other students, during which professors and successful entrepreneurs run workshops on business ownership. Then after graduating, participants have access to a year's worth of technical assistance from program faculty.

From the point of application to the close of the technical assistance period, each student costs EBV $5,280. Thanks to philanthropic gifts and in-kind donations from the sponsor universities, participants do not pay a dime. EBV keeps costs low by running the administration and program planning out of the Institute for Veterans and Military Families, the organization JPMorgan Chase has funded at Syracuse University (See pages 59–61).

To ensure that every student receives the same high-quality teaching, EBV trains instructors from each of its university partners at Syracuse, and provides them with all of the teaching materials necessary. Every university is, in turn, responsible for donating space, technology resources, and teaching staff. Large universities with successful business schools have been lining up to participate, but because of Haynie's determination to keep program standards high and bureaucracy and costs low, he is reluctant to expand much beyond the current reach of the program.

Teaching Charities to Prioritize Veterans

Robin Hood Foundation leads good service providers to a new population

The Robin Hood Foundation is an unusual creature. It is a master fundraiser—annually collecting more than $120 million in donations which it then grants to New York City–based nonprofits. Appealing mostly to hedge-fund managers and Wall Street financiers, the group shifts money (as its name implies) from the wealthy to the poor.

Robin Hood does not run programs itself, but pursues its goals by making grants to nonprofit organizations. Yet it has very detailed ideas of how problems ought to be solved, and often exerts its influence even more through the detailed management assistance and hard-headed strategic advice it bundles with its grants than from the substantial size of the checks it writes. The organization is at once a donor and an exacting social-services advisory organization.

And Robin Hood is tightly focused. First, its sole area of operations is New York City. Second, poverty reduction is at the center of most of its initiatives. When it decides to act in a sector like public health or early childhood education, it does so with an explicit anti-poverty rationale.

Amidst many temptations to drift into adjoining causes and locales, the foundation has shown considerable mission discipline since its founding in 1988. Periodically, though, Robin Hood does take on new ways of battling poverty. Its most recent expansion has been to take on obstacles to the economic flourishing of veterans as they re-enter civilian society.

Making Veterans a Priority

In January 2011, Adm. Michael Mullen, then the chairman of the Pentagon's Joint Chiefs of Staff, approached Robin Hood and asked it to become a leader in helping veterans resettle into their home communities. Despite the tidal wave of public money now being channeled to veterans (between 2004 and 2012, the budget for the Department of Veterans Affairs alone more than doubled from $62 billion to nearly $127 billion) healthy homecomings require a community response as much as a federal one.

Robin Hood accepted the challenge. It formed an advisory board chaired by Mullen and hedge-fund manager Steven Cohen, who has a personal interest in the subject as father to an enlisted Marine. The new initiative raised $13.1 million to fund its initial grantmaking. As of January 2013, Robin Hood had distributed about $7 million to 24 programs serving veterans, servicemembers, and their families.

The territory was not entirely new for Robin Hood. Eric Weingartner, head of the foundation's work in this area, explains, "We have been serving veterans for 25 years, though not deliberately as a sub-population." So instead of dreaming up an entirely new program, "we spent a lot of time with the V.A., the city, nonprofits, and veterans organizations trying to figure out the landscape" and then applied the Robin Hood model to the particular needs of military veterans and their families.

They kept their focus on New York City and on fighting poverty. "We've been approached by hundreds of groups, and we've met some that are incredibly well-meaning and might even be effective. But we didn't fund them because our program is focused on local veterans living in poverty. While we're sympathetic to many other programs, our mission is to serve New Yorkers and deliver human-services outcomes."

In the process of becoming knowledgeable about what veterans need to avoid economic failure, Weingartner admits, "we have been part of thousands of conversations with nonprofits that didn't lead anywhere." Yet as the foundation zeroed in on areas where it had expertise and a mandate linked to the foundation's wider mission, it gradually had fewer misfires. "We're not chasing something that's elusive to us."

Robin Hood has recognized that there are ways in which veterans having trouble finding economic success are different from other poor populations. Certain of the obstacles it faces are unique. Some of the strengths it has to build on are different.

> The Robin Hood Foundation zeroed in
> on areas where it already had
> social-services expertise.

"Our aim is to find the best-in-class program for a particular problem" and then apply it across different populations, notes Kimberly Smith, Weingartner's second-in-command on the veterans initiative. But tools that work with single mothers, or non-English speakers, or substance abusers, or the under-educated, will often not be useful for struggling veterans. So, Smith reports, "we asked, 'What are the veterans' unique needs?' Then we found interventions targeting that."

The first step was to intelligently narrow the population funnel. Robin Hood estimates that there are about 250,000 veterans living in New York City. At most, one-tenth of these are veterans of the wars in Iraq and Afghanistan. And only a minority of these new veterans would benefit from Robin Hood's economic programs. Most vets, as data throughout this book illustrates, will succeed quite handsomely on their own.

But several thousand New York City veterans might benefit from Robin Hood's programs, and with this target population in mind, Weingartner and Smith have funded programs addressing employment, mental health, education, housing, legal services, and other topics. All are informed by what the foundation has learned in 25 years of poverty-fighting with other populations in New York City.

Working around Interest Groups and Governments

Weingartner and Smith learned early on the importance of military cultural competence. They couldn't serve—or even find—populations in need without help from individuals or groups with experience in the specialized language, economic history, and social experiences that can be peculiar to military life. On the other hand, many veterans organizations "couldn't produce the outcomes that Robin Hood measures—like jobs, health care, and housing," says Weingartner. Most were startups with no infrastructure, track record, or ability to forecast how a six-figure grant from Robin Hood would concretely improve the lives of New Yorkers. Weingartner was not willing to place large bets on infrastructure that was only imagined or promised.

Instead, the foundation sought to bring existing social-work competencies of their home city to bear on this new population. "New York is a human-services town," asserts Weingartner, with many experienced practitioners already at work across the metro area. The end result, according to Weingartner: "Most of the organizations we're funding are not exclusively veterans organizations; they're social-service agencies that have expanded to serve vets."

After determining what services veterans most needed, and which groups had the best track-record in that area, Robin Hood then paid these groups to prioritize vets and their families. Most often, this translated into hiring staff specifically focused on finding and serving the relevant men, women, and children.

This got the city's most effective social-service nonprofits into the habit of thinking about veterans, understanding how they differ from others, and how they can be helped to succeed. That *teaches* organizations, so that even after Robin Hood's special funding for veterans winds down, charities will be likelier to remember this special population in the course of their general operations. And through its four permanent grantmaking portfolios—education, jobs and economic security, survival, and early childhood and youth—the Robin Hood Foundation will continue to help citizens with military service records even if it's not operating separate veterans programming.

Weingartner also notes the importance of recognizing the influence of the governmental elephants in the room: "Our instinct was to support and augment government from the beginning." When working within the social-service bureaucracy in a city like New York, though, or with the national benefit programs run by the U.S. Department of Veterans Affairs, successful nonprofits must be smart:

> We went right to city hall. What is the Mayor's Office of Veterans Affairs? What do the housing programs do for vets? What does welfare do for vets? What is happening on the public-health side for vets? We figured out the landscape and then started to invent in concert with nonprofits and the city.

The foundation worked to immediately serve vets. It also helped others learn how to serve them. A donor working in this way can thus be "a catalyst" as well as a solver of problems on his own.

Achieving Cultural Competency

Supplementing proven, existing programs makes intervention cheaper, and increases the likelihood that effective services will be delivered. That said, teaching an organization to understand military culture and reach veterans is no small matter. A group that has had great success with immigrants or high-school dropouts might lack the instincts and capacities needed to be effective with men and women coming out of the military.

Robin Hood requires its grantees to explain how they will acquire competence with servicemembers. Weingartner has seen all kinds of adaptations. "We made the bet that our grantees could learn to serve veterans. In some cases it's hiring; in some cases it's training; in some cases it's program development; in some cases, it's curricula."

Adding new tools to reach veterans can have overflow effects. For instance, Robin Hood funded a homelessness program to increase its outreach teams from 2.5 people per borough to 3.5—asking the extra personnel to particularly strive to identify and prioritize homeless veterans. The program took 200 veterans off the street in one year, as well as other individuals reached by the extra manpower.

Robin Hood has increased efficiency by requiring its veterans grantees to refer clients to one another whenever appropriate. The foundation developed a website through which organizations could send individuals to each other. It required all of its grantees to meet each other face-to-face several months into the grant cycle, to encourage information- and client-sharing.

Sometimes it's little things that allow one program to succeed while a similar one languishes. One of Robin Hood's first mental-health grants aimed to provide free counseling services to the 50 percent of veterans who have not registered for V.A. benefits, and to family members of veterans (who are not eligible for V.A. health benefits, though they bear their own burdens from deployment). The clinic ultimately served only half as many clients as expected, though, so Robin Hood discontinued that kind of work.

Robin Hood demands accountability. It has begun funding its grantees in installments based on their ability to hit recruitment goals. This creates incentives for grantees to solve their problems quickly, and it lets Robin Hood nimbly redirect funding to its best vendors. If programs don't improve and meet their goals, the foundation can pull funding altogether.

"In developing veterans programs," says Weingartner, "we applied the same rigorous metrics as we did to regular Robin Hood programs. We evaluate the value of interventions. We attach grant dollars to very specific outcomes and ask grantees to demonstrate that the money was used effectively."

The Lilly Endowment Goes to Work in Its Own Back Yard

Another large donor that, like Robin Hood, chose to keep a local focus while addressing the needs of veterans, servicemembers, and their families is the Lilly Endowment. Lilly got involved ahead of many other groups. In 2007, it made four large grants in support of military populations across Indiana (a state whose military units are primarily National Guard). The Indiana National Guard Relief Fund received $570,000 to address service-connected financial hardship among military families, plus programs for military children. Crane Technology received $400,000 for a pilot program to rehabilitate and train around 20 disabled veterans.

The largest grant, $9.9 million, went to the Richard Roudebush V.A. Medical Center in Indianapolis (one of the V.A.'s 21 polytrauma centers). The grant funds a clinic that aims to house all the services most patients would need under one roof—primary care, mental health, social work, and vocational rehabilitation, plus a 28-suite residence for families of servicemembers undergoing treatment. The aim is to make it easier for patients to get what they need without jumping inter-office hurdles.

The fourth Lilly grant, of $8.9 million, went to the Purdue University Military Family Research Institute (MFRI). Shelley MacDermid Wadsworth, MFRI's director, explains that

> MFRI does not emphasize direct service. We're focused on trying to help practitioners already in the field do their work more effectively. We create connections between programs and work to embed intellectual capital in systems that already exist. It's inspiring that Lilly understood that—they value community-based work which often does not generate big headlines about jazzy programs, but instead requires a lot of behind-the-scenes work in the trenches.

MFRI re-granted more than $2.5 million of Lilly's investment to other institutions of higher education in Indiana, to support student veterans and servicemembers, and encourage schools to experiment with different ways of helping them succeed in their studies.

EDUCATION

Bolstering a Decentralized Success

Gates builds a data backbone for Student Veterans of America

Student veteran organizations have existed at colleges across America for decades. In the years immediately following World War II, the Korean War, and the conflict in Vietnam, large influxes of veterans onto college campuses turned institutions of higher learning into institutions of re-integration as well. As the wars in Iraq and Afghanistan wound down, the ranks of student veteran organizations began to swell again.

In early 2008, student leaders from 20 local student veteran organizations from throughout the country gathered together in Chicago to found Student Veterans of America (SVA). The founders "recognized that there was greater potential for these groups to support the student veteran population if they coalesced under one banner," says Matt Feger, director of development for the group.

SVA remains a chapter-based organization, which keeps it easy for new local chapters to spring up and to organize their affairs in their own way. The only requirements are that each group register as a student organization on its campus, obtain an advisor at the school, and have one veteran point of contact. Rather than forcing chapters into one mold, the national headquarters works with each to improve their operations and serve their local members as effectively as possible.

And members differ from other students in some important ways. As Feger summarizes:

> They come to school with very different life experiences than the 18-year-old coming straight out of high school. They are much older. Many are first-generation college students. Many have families already. And many have just come back from a war that was different from any others that we've been in. They are trying to simultaneously adjust to life as a civilian and to life as a student. Schools weren't really prepared for that.

In four years, SVA has grown from 20 chapters to more than 700, spanning all 50 states. Local branches have succeeded at shaping campus policies, training chapter members, awarding scholarships, and advocating for student veterans in the public sphere. For example, in 2010, the SVA chapter leader from Florida State University wrote a business plan that convinced the university to invest in veterans. The graduation rate of veterans at FSU climbed to 86 percent, and the university committed to building a 30,000-square-foot veterans center on campus.

The Gates Foundation Builds a Strong Backbone

Just as SVA was experiencing its meteoric rise in membership, Margot Tyler, then an officer for college programs at the Bill & Melinda Gates Foundation, became interested in veterans as a target population. "With the implementation of the new G.I. Bill, I knew there were a lot of opportunities available for veterans, but that those opportunities were not being fully exploited." In particular, many vets did not complete their degree on time. Tyler set a philanthropic goal to "remove barriers to college completion for veteran students."

She began an intensive process to find the right service provider for the Gates Foundation to partner with. She conducted informal focus groups with

> Student Veterans of America has hundreds of local branches that help shape campus policies, award scholarships, and advocate for student veterans.

current student veterans, had conversations with institutions of higher learning, and conducted research on potential grantees ranging from think tanks to national education associations. Ultimately, because of SVA's direct ties to student veterans themselves and great potential for growth, Tyler became convinced that SVA would be the best steward of a 2011 grant to move student veterans toward degree completion.

"Once we identified SVA," explains Tyler, "it was all about working with them as partners to develop a growth plan." Tyler saw that Student Veterans of America was a young organization with a lean staff that had relied primarily on the passion and energy of volunteers. For its next stage she urged that they get some professional help. Together, Gates and SVA chose the consulting group Bridgespan to help formulate future strategy.

From the level of 400 chapters when Gates paid for this consulting work, Student Veterans of America has since exceeded 700 chapters. And the growth has been carefully managed. "We collectively decided," says Feger, "on five strategic initiatives, on a staff growth plan, and on a steady-state budget." SVA strengthened itself in a few key areas: It now provides some small grants to its local chapters. It holds training sessions for its student leaders. It hosts national conferences to help members spread ideas between chapters. And it is collaborating with Purdue University's Military Family Research Institute to create a manual for chapter activities.

The strengthened and professionalized Student Veterans of America also began to generate crucial statistics on the college paths of today's veterans. No reliable estimate of the graduation rate of veterans using the Post-9/11 G.I. Bill existed. So SVA began working with the administrators of G.I. Bill spending, and with the National Student Clearinghouse. The clearinghouse knows who completes a degree, transfers, or drops out of college, and by matching that with student information from the administrators of the G.I. Bill, the first good data on exactly which veterans are succeeding or failing, and at what types of academic institutions, will eventually become available. This factual background will be of great future value to all parties interested in helping veterans succeed.

First Learn, Then Teach
Walmart and Kresge help a nonprofit organize colleges

The American Council on Education (ACE) began offering support to veterans and servicemembers on college campuses long before the wars in Iraq and Afghanistan. The organization was founded in 1918 to help address the higher-education needs of returning American servicemembers in the wake of World War I. After World War II and the passage of the nation's first G.I. Bill, the council intensified its work. Over the years, ACE has expanded beyond these military-related programs into topics like lifelong learning, college affordability, diversity, effective administration, and the internationalization of education. Today, its membership includes approximately 1,600 colleges and universities, and 200 college associations.

One of the early achievements of ACE was helping servicemembers receive certain forms of academic credit for their military learning. Rather than apply a single set of standards, ACE developed two programs that have since become standards in higher education: the General Education Development (GED) testing program, which certifies that individuals have all of the requisite skills taught in a traditional high school curriculum, and the *Military Guide*, which provides institutions of higher learning with recommendations for awarding course credit for particular forms of military training.

In recent years, with the passage of the Post-9/11 G.I. Bill, the most generous educational benefit for veterans since World War II, ACE members noticed an influx of veterans into their classrooms. Colleges and universities turned to ACE for help identifying promising practices that could support these new students in their studies. Although ACE's *Military Guide* remained a useful tool for converting military experience to course credit, "higher education knows that the education experience is about more than just sitting down in a classroom," says Meg Mitcham, the current director of veterans programs at ACE.

And so, in 2008, ACE began a new initiative to "provide programs and services to institutions of higher education to help them ensure that today's veterans are college and career ready," in Mitcham's words. Rather than developing this from scratch, ACE borrowed from its existing programs on educating older students, and leaned on the in-house team that had long been working with the various service branches on the *Military Guide* for training-to-coursework conversion. Two specific programs were created: the Success for Veterans Award Grants, and the Veterans Success Jam.

Funded by the Walmart Foundation, the Success for Veterans Award Grants provided $100,000 to each of 20 colleges around the country (selected from 248 applicants) to serve as laboratories for veteran support in higher education. The program aims to "explore existing programs and initiatives supporting student veterans, promote awareness of innovative ideas and lessons learned, and disseminate insights and ideas to institutions of higher learning."

These grants began in June 2009 and ended with a final report in July 2011. Mitcham explains, "We funded those grants with the hope of really understanding the process these institutions went through, what challenges they hit, and how they addressed them." To what extent these programs would succeed in those early days was uncertain.

Many colleges are hungry to know what they can do to make themselves open to veterans.

When Mitcham set out on site visits to each of the grantees, however, what she discovered surprised her. "I wasn't sure what these programs would look like, or how much they would differ. But at 20 institutions I found 20 drastically different programs, all of which were highly successful. It became clear very quickly that there was no single definition of what 'veteran-friendly' meant." Fresno City College, for instance, built a job-training pipeline into major regional employer Pacific Gas & Electric, while the CUNY Silberman School of Social Work hired and trained student interns to support veterans.

To make sure they stayed closely in touch with what different sorts of campuses were learning and needing, ACE organized a Veterans Success Jam with support from the Kresge Foundation. "We wanted to be sure we heard the viewpoints of all of our member institutions—two-year and four-year institutions, public and private institutions, rural and urban ones, institutions located in close proximity to military bases and ones that weren't," says Mitcham. Gathering feedback from 1,600 institutions plus other stakeholders was a big undertaking, but ACE managed by hosting the Veteran Success Jam as a "three-day online brainstorming event." Organized around seven major discussion topics and several training webcasts, the event attracted 2,877 registrants.

Throughout the Jam, participants returned again and again to the phrase "veteran and military friendly." Yet nobody really knew what that meant. Colleges were hungry to know what they should do to make themselves open and useful to veterans. Answering that became the next phase of ACE's work.

Turning Research into Action

ACE made it their goal to "take everything we learned over the past few years and help the rest of the institutions out there, whether they are our members or not." In addition to the vast amount of information and experience collected from the Jam and grant awards, colleges continually approached ACE to share their new and evolving programs. Realizing that what worked for one institution may not work at the next, Mitcham and colleagues decided to offer options:

> We needed to help institutions see that there are multiple ways of addressing any of these issues, and we needed to provide them with

examples of those. We'll give them the program and the guide, but there are many different ways they could turn and still successfully serve their military and veteran students.

With this in mind, ACE built the Toolkit for Veteran-Friendly Institutions. It is more a collection of case studies and samples than a set of prescriptions for colleges and universities to follow. In more than a dozen categories, the Toolkit diagnoses the challenges student veterans face, then provides documents and resources used by various universities to solve those problems. It provides, for just a few examples, a copy of Wayne State University's veterans housing policy, an agenda from the University of Illinois' veterans orientation program, and an overview of Central Michigan University's training given to professors working with veterans. As of early 2013, 529 institutions of higher learning have registered for the Toolkit.

All of this information exchanging seems to be improving campus offerings. According to ACE's Soldier to Student surveys—one conducted in 2009 and the other in 2012, bracketing ACE's Jam and the Veteran Success Award Grants—the percentage of schools providing special programming for veterans increased from 57 percent to 62 percent nationwide, and the number of institutions saying such programming is a priority increased from 57 percent to 71 percent.

As with others in this relatively new field, ACE began its work by conducting research and running pilot programs. Once it began to understand the full spectrum of issues facing veterans on campus, and the institutions wanting to cater to them, the group began to put that research to work. While acknowledging that there is no single solution, ACE's Toolkit offers well-organized lessons and examples that can be used by motivated institutions of higher education to welcome and better serve the influx of veterans they can expect over the next several years.

Welcoming Veterans to Elite Campuses

Companies pay Posse to extend a proven model

We are committed to bringing to campus a diverse group of students who will learn from each other. Different life experiences and different opinions contribute to the learning that takes place on campus. . . . Greater understanding between the civilian and military spheres of our society has to be good for our country.
—Catharine Bond Hill, president, Vassar College

The military calls it a squad. The Posse Foundation calls it, well, a posse. It is a group of about 10 individuals who work with and depend on one another to accomplish a mission. In more than one setting, small groups like this have the potential to make the seemingly insurmountable possible.

In 1989, long before it had any relation to the military, the idea for the Posse method struck Debbie Bial, the organization's founder and president. She had heard a student say, "I never would have dropped out of college if I had my posse with me." The initial focus of the foundation was on creating social supports at top colleges that would reduce dropout rates among students from poor urban neighborhoods.

Posse aimed to solve two problems at once. First, although many elite colleges were anxious to have low-income and minority students on their campuses, they found it difficult to get them and keep them in school. Second, students from these backgrounds often failed to complete their degrees in spite of generous scholarship packages.

Bial's solution was simple—instead of bringing in these students as isolated enrollees, recruit a group (or posse) from the same place and background and help them reinforce each other as they made the transition to a new social world. Beginning with a unique, team-oriented recruitment model, Posse works with universities to identify 10 high-potential high-school seniors from a single city who might not otherwise consider a top-flight university for cultural or economic reasons. Once selected, the posse undergoes eight months of pre-college training in teamwork, academics, and leadership, motivated by a full scholarship guarantee from the host college.

The members of the posse thus get to know one another well long before they arrive on campus, and they continue to meet as a group once enrolled. They receive weekly mentorship from campus liaisons and Posse staff throughout their four years of undergraduate study. And as they approach graduation, Posse provides them with internship opportunities, an alumni network, and career counseling. Since its founding, Posse has sent 4,237 students from nine cities to 44 top-tier colleges, secured nearly $500 million in scholarships for those students, and graduated them at a rate of 90 percent.

Extending an Existing Success

Since 2009, Vassar College had participated in the Yellow Ribbon Program— an extension of the Post-9/11 G.I. Bill through which expensive private colleges offer veterans extra scholarships, matched by veterans benefits, dramatically lowering the cost of enrollment. Despite this offer, though, "we hadn't been having any luck getting veterans into our applicant pool," reports Vassar president Catharine Hill. Several years into the program, Vassar had only one veteran on campus.

In January 2012, Hill and Bial were talking by phone about Posse's new program for inner-city students interested in the sciences. It occurred to Hill that Posse's model might also work "in both recruiting veterans and supporting them through college." She floated the idea with Bial, to whom it made immediate sense. Before the end of the month, Posse's board of directors had approved the idea of extending their program with the aim of getting more veterans onto the campuses of elite colleges, and then keeping them there until graduation.

A few weeks later, the most important element fell into place. Major philanthropic support was offered. The organization secured lead funding from Infor, a software company, plus six-figure donations from other donors like Goldman Sachs, JPMorgan Chase, Moody's, and Viacom.

A few months later, Posse opened the nominations process. By the end of 2012 it had selected its first class of scholars; 150 veterans were considered for just 11 spots. The foundation hopes to be sending posses of veterans to 10 top colleges in the near future.

Hill recognized that it wasn't necessary to invent a new organization to solve Vassar's problem in bringing vets to selective colleges and universities. She saw several qualities in the existing Posse formula, which had evolved over two decades, that could be redirected to this new population. "First, the Posse Foundation has a way to successfully identify talented candidates who will succeed in college. It was proving difficult for each individual school, like Vassar, with fairly small admissions offices, to encourage veterans to get into our applicant pools. Posse does this exceptionally well, and can do it for lots of schools as the program expands."

Second, there seemed to be a natural fit between veterans and the small-group, mutual-support ethic on which Posse relies. Bial explains, "The idea that students will thrive if they go to college 'with their posse' seemed very relevant for veterans. In particular, everything we knew suggested that veterans wanted to be someplace where there were others who had had similar experiences. They know how to work in a team, they always have each other's backs,

Posse operates on the principle that the support of peers in small groups can make possible the seemingly insurmountable.

they're disciplined, they're motivated. And yet these are very non-traditional students for these campuses—their average age is 27 and they're going to campuses and living with 18-year-olds."

Once on campus, veterans in each posse will receive the same level of support as all posses do. Posse remains humble about its foray into serving a new population, and recognizes it may need to revise its formula in places. "What will be different is that vets are at a different place in their lives—they're older, more mature, and have very different kinds of experiences the past few years of their lives. We have to acknowledge that in our programming."

Among the adaptations already made is replacement of the eight-month pre-college training with a one-month intensive residential course. It takes place in New York City, and accommodates posse members from all over the country. With the support of donors, Posse aims to expand the program to serve 500 students per year.

Mastering the Private-public Partnership

The Fisher family's several triumphs in catalyzing medical and family care

When it comes to philanthropy supporting veterans, servicemembers, and their families, the Fisher family represents the gold standard. They were in the field before almost anyone else. Their projects have been soaringly successful. And they have managed to repeat their triumphs—first in one area, then in another, later in third and fourth sectors.

It is difficult to summarize on a few pages the size and breadth of the Fisher family's giving to the military, but the highlight reel looks something like this: They turned a retired aircraft carrier into a floating museum of military history dedicated to those who have served (doing this in New York City, no less, where they had to overcome many regulatory obstacles). They built 58 comfort homes with private funds, to house injured servicemembers and their families during extended treatments at V.A. or Department of Defense medical facilities; these homes have so far provided more than 4.7 million days of free housing to these stressed families. At a time when the Fishers considered the "death benefits" paid by the government to families of fallen servicemembers to be insufficient, they supplemented those payments with private charitable funds. To improve the rehabilitation of combat amputees, the Fishers built a 60,000 square foot rehabilitation center that has redefined the state of the art. And most recently, the Fisher family began building a network of privately funded traumatic stress and brain injury research and treatment centers on V.A. and Department of Defense medical campuses around the country.

This work was carried out through several different giving vehicles— the Intrepid Museum Foundation, the Zachary and Elizabeth M. Fisher Armed Services Foundation, the Fisher House Foundation, and the Intrepid Fallen Heroes Fund. And the Fishers recruited hundreds of funding partners to finance these charitable activities. But the family has consistently put organizing energy as well as money into these ventures, and their contributions have evolved over time in very savvy ways to remain relevant to the needs of veterans and members of the military as circumstances have changed.

One thing remains constant through each of these engagements, a factor that is likely be the family's major philanthropic legacy. The Fishers pioneered a unique and exemplary take on the private-public partnership. Indeed they managed to take the traditional private-public collaboration—within which the influence of philanthropy is often swamped by the demands of the government—and stand it on its head. Rather than letting large and inflexible public institutions call the tune, the Fishers managed to wield their private philanthropy as a prod to get the public sector to act in much more entrepreneurial ways.

There is constant talk in the world of philanthropy about "private-public partnerships." In many cases, however, this devolves into government officials and bureaucracies setting the rules and then trying to get private entities to cut the check. A lot of these efforts—for instance when taken up in traditional public-school systems—have turned out to be disappointing and dysfunctional. A private-public partnership in the Fisher philanthropy, however, is a different beast. Under their model, the private partner has been the instigator, planner, agenda-maker, setter of the schedule, and energy source. The private donors have solved launch issues the government was too cumbersome to sort out, and then they've held their public partners to account for timely follow-through.

A Long History, Not a Flash in the Pan

Zachary Fisher initiated the family's charitable work on behalf of members of the military. Born in 1910 to Jewish immigrants from Lithuania, he dropped out of high school at the age of 16 to work as a bricklayer, joining his brothers Martin and Larry in the family business of general contracting. Soon, they formed a new real-estate business in New York City, Fisher Brothers, through which they would eventually build or manage more than 10 million square feet of prime space in the city, and make the fortune that has allowed their decades-long philanthropy to flourish.

After the bombing of Pearl Harbor, Zachary tried to enlist in the U.S. Marine Corps but was denied because of a knee injury he had incurred while working construction. Instead, he offered his services to the U.S. Army Corps of Engineers to help construct coastal fortifications at home. His wife, Elizabeth, served in the USO, entertaining troops with the Ziegfeld Follies.

They continued their commitment to the well-being of members of our armed forces through various projects in the 1950s, 1960s, and 1970s, until they embarked on their first major philanthropic project: saving the USS *Intrepid* from becoming scrap metal, turning it instead into the Intrepid Sea, Air, and Space Museum, a place where children and adults in New York City could develop a richer appreciation of military service. In addition to putting up $25 million of his own money for the project, Fisher worked to pass an act of Congress to purchase the carrier, and to rewrite New York City building codes to harbor it in the then-economically depressed Hell's Kitchen district. By 1982 the Intrepid Museum was open for business, and soon after it became an entirely self-sustaining endeavor.

After the 1983 bombing of U.S. Marine barracks in Beirut, Zachary and Elizabeth Fisher created the Intrepid Fallen Heroes Fund to support the families of slain servicemembers. Though the government provided one-time cash transfers to these families, the Fishers felt they were insufficient. So they began giving as much as $25,000 in supplemental gifts directly to families. They continued distributing these until 2005, when the government significantly increased its own contributions to the survivors of the fallen.

Focusing on What They Do Best

In 1990, Zachary and Elizabeth Fisher contacted Adm. Carlisle Trost, Chief of Naval Operations, to ask how they might expand their support for families of wounded servicemembers. Trost relayed an issue that had concerned his wife, Pauline, for some time: the lack of affordable housing for out-of-town family members visiting wounded servicemembers on their way to recovery. Many families must travel long distances from their homes to help care for loved ones recovering for days, weeks, or months in V.A. and Defense Department medical facilities. These sojourns in strange cities often presented serious financial and emotional hardships for family members.

After hearing the story of a young sailor who slept in his car while his wife received treatment at a DoD hospital, the Fishers decided to act, with Zachary famously saying, "I'm a builder, I have my own architect, we can do this." With their own $20 million investment, the Fishers created the Fisher House Foundation. The idea of providing homes away from home where families can stay while their servicemembers medically recuperate was simple. Implementation was not as easy.

The Fishers required that no family ever be charged for its stay at a Fisher House. They also stipulated that the houses had to be within walking distance of the medical facilities they were meant to serve—which generally meant building on government-owned land. Zachary Fisher knew his limits—he was a gifted builder, not a hotel manager—so he insisted that some other entity had to actually manage the houses once they were erected.

Developing the houses would have been a multi-year bureaucratic and budgetary ordeal for the federal government, "but we could build them faster, for lower costs, and with extremely high quality, ultimately saving the government millions of dollars" says Zachary's great-nephew Ken Fisher, chairman of the Fisher House Foundation. It was much more feasible for the Departments of Defense and Veterans Affairs to provide land, ongoing maintenance and operation, and property management, especially with the added incentive of getting the fully furnished comfort home for free. Says Fisher, "It was just a natural step to build them as gifts and proffer them to the government, which would fold them into the base and military culture so they could do what they do best, which is operate and staff them."

Once the deal was struck, Zachary Fisher brought in architects and construction partners to build the first two Fisher Houses at Walter Reed Army Medical Center and National Naval Medical Center. On their completion in 1991, Fisher proffered the buildings to the Department of Defense, and the Fisher Houses were open for business.

> Fisher Houses provide more than just a place for caretakers to rest at the end of long days of recovery—they provide community.

Since then, the Fishers built another 58 houses, including one abroad (for families of wounded British soldiers at Queen Elizabeth Hospital in the United Kingdom), and new houses continue to open as this is written. Each house consists of anywhere from 8 to 21 suites, with shared kitchen space, laundry facilities, dining room, library, and living room, in a 5,000 to 16,000 square-foot edifice. In 2012 alone, the houses served 19,000 different families. The nearly 5 million days of free lodging they have provided have saved families hundreds of millions of dollars in food, lodging, and transportation expenses.

Fisher Houses provide more than just a place for caretakers to rest their heads at the end of long days of recovery. One of the effects of housing these families together has been the inherent sense of community and shared experience. Worried and grieving families are brought together in a supportive and comforting environment where concerns and joys can be shared with others facing the same circumstances. The homes have proved wondrously popular.

Through this carefully structured private-public partnership, private philanthropy was able to motivate government to quickly provide a service that it was failing to provide on its own. Government was able to expand its care for servicemembers and their families with much-reduced startup costs and bureaucratic effort. And American families in distress benefited greatly.

Once established, the Fisher Houses became an entry point for other private philanthropy in the notoriously difficult-to-access worlds of the V.A. and DoD. In 2005, the Fisher Houses and DoD began administering a Hero Miles program through which seven airlines allow passengers to donate their frequent-flyer miles to provide free tickets to servicemembers receiving medical care who are ineligible for government reimbursement, plus family and close friends visiting injured servicemembers during their recovery. Since its inception, the program has provided over 30,000 tickets collectively valued at more than $45 million.

Administered similarly, the Hotels for Heroes program provides free lodging to these populations at 17 hotel chains. The Returning Heroes Home Foundation was able to form a similar private-public partnership to build the Warrior and Family Support Center, a privately funded 12,000 square-foot assistance and recreation center on the campus of the San Antonio Military Medical Center in Texas.

Far More Than Lodging

After Zachary Fisher's death in 1999, the rest of the Fisher family continued to expand their philanthropic work in support of servicemembers, veterans, and their families. In addition to continually building new Fisher Houses to keep up with injuries from the wars in Afghanistan and Iraq, the Fishers became involved in the medical treatment process itself. As with the Fisher Houses, the family offered a jump-start by providing expertise, energy, and startup funding.

Under the leadership of Tony and Arnold Fisher (Zachary's nephews), the Fishers' medical work first focused on those with major amputations or extensive burns—soldiers who likely would have died in previous wars with less advanced battlefield medicine, and who now needed long-term rehabilitation and prosthetic help. After the government increased death benefits for families of fallen servicemembers in 2005, Arnold Fisher led the family to repurpose the Intrepid Fallen Heroes Fund for this new cause. By January 2007, the fund had raised $55 million from 600,000 donors and completed construction of the Center for the Intrepid. Located next to two Fisher Houses on the campus of the San Antonio Military Medical Center, this gleaming 65,000 square-foot facility treats about 140 gravely wounded patients, in a total of about 600 appointments, in any typical week. Like the Fisher Houses, once the foundation had planned, built, and equipped the center, it was proffered to the government for staffing, maintenance, and programming.

With its focus on serving those with amputations, severe burns, or functional limb loss, the Center for the Intrepid brings under one roof prosthetic fitting and fabrication, behavioral medicine, and physical and occupational therapy. Patients receive intensive treatment from teams of professionals working together to address the patient comprehensively, rather than one malady at a time. Supplemented by state-of-the-art technology and adaptive sports equipment, treatment plans allow patients to learn to walk again, to take care of themselves, to play sports, even to reacquaint themselves with their old military work and weapons systems.

Although the V.A. and DoD have many fine medical facilities and programs, the privately funded Center for the Intrepid offered several advantages. First, as with the Fisher Houses, private funding and building services allowed the center to be open and aiding badly wounded men and women years before would otherwise have been possible. Moreover, the center enabled the military medical system to bring a wide range of medical professionals under one roof to provide integrated care that would previously have required multiple visits to multiple facilities. The Intrepid Fallen Heroes Fund didn't simply donate a new building, it demanded and facilitated the reorganization of resources within the Defense Department to better serve patients.

Building for Brain Health

After cutting the ribbon at the Center for the Intrepid, the Fisher family quickly reoriented toward a new problem: mental and brain health in the military. Post-traumatic stress and brain injuries are not new to the wars in Iraq and Afghanistan, any more than multiple amputations, severe burns, and functional limb loss are new. But as more routine medical problems are solved by improving medicine, these trickier effects of combat are now a major focus of military medical care.

Recognizing how difficult it can be to diagnose and treat brain injuries and traumatic stress, the Fishers decided to invest in that area. Although the military had excellent physicians, "the need for a center of excellence that

> The Intrepid Fallen Heroes Fund catalyzed the reorganization of resources within the Defense Department to better serve patients.

could both conduct research and treat patients had become critical," says Ken Fisher. Following the model they had pioneered with both Fisher Houses and the Center for the Intrepid, the Fishers decided to create a facility that could elevate care for neurological issues in the way San Antonio's Center for the Intrepid had improved amputation therapy. Arnold Fisher set about meeting with doctors all over the country to determine what such a facility might need in terms of space, equipment, and other requirements.

Initially, the military was nervous about the idea—"like anyone, they want to be able to take care of their own," says Ken Fisher, "but we weren't looking to take over or take away, we were looking to complement what was being done." They warmed up to it quickly and a facility was planned for the Walter Reed National Military Medical Center campus in Bethesda, Maryland. It was dubbed the National Intrepid Center of Excellence, or NICoE (pronounced "nigh-coh").

Officially proffered to the Department of the Navy in June 2010, NICoE is a 72,000 square-foot facility carrying out research, diagnosis, and treatment on brain injuries and stress disorders with injured servicemembers and veterans. Over the course of four weeks at NICoE, patients undergo evaluations by a team of medical professionals—sometimes more than a dozen—that diagnose problems and develop a treatment program for the patient's entire family. After evaluation, NICoE physicians work with the patient's home doctor to coordinate the treatment plan.

Since completing NICoE, the Intrepid Fallen Heroes Fund has embarked on a project to build as many as six more NICoE satellite centers around the country, so patients can be treated as close as possible to their homes. Explaining the rationale behind these, Ken Fisher says: "You don't just receive treatment and walk out. It has to be ongoing—the satellite centers are meant to get patients home as quickly as possible so they can receive treatment there, while monitoring their progress." Each of these $11 million NICoE satellite clinics will provide evaluations and treatment, and train healthcare providers. The local clinics will conduct some research, but as they open the facility in Bethesda will become the primary center for evaluations and research.

How does a philanthropic family with experience constructing and managing real estate come to instigate solutions to complex medical problems like amputations, burns, brain injury, and traumatic stress? The same way as it addressed the hardships faced by family members caring for their injured loved ones. By focusing attention on the problem, quickly building top-of-the-line facilities where those in need could be treated, all the while pressing the responsible government bureaucracies to create staff and plans to solve the problems, and then turning over the keys for professionals to run the place. Essentially, the Fishers defined the issues, then set up a dynamic where it would be too painful for the government to fail to address them, and relatively easy to accomplish good new things.

Getting Beyond the Buzzword in Private-public Partnerships

It was a great advantage for the Fishers that they had a nearly 20-year track record of working with the military before the war on terror magnified problems of the sort they wanted to solve. That earlier experience unquestionably enhanced their ability to ramp up creative private-public partnerships where private philanthropy was the driving force, not the lagging influence. Nonetheless, the sheer programmatic diversity, geographic spread, and consistent excellence of their good works is so unparalleled in the world of philanthropy that it's clear there were also some very smart strategy decisions being made, quite apart from their advantages of experience.

In the Fisher family's work with DoD and V.A., the private donors never simply write a check to pay the government to provide services. Nor does private philanthropy dream up and demand a project that would eventually become a burden on government resources better spent elsewhere. The Fishers avoided both of those dead ends.

Instead, their work has allowed both the philanthropists and their necessary public partners to bring their specialties and strengths to the table. And the private donors have, somewhat inexplicably, managed to avoid letting the bureaucratic blob overwhelm them. The philanthropists provided the motivating force and essential marching orders that allowed fresh solutions to emerge. And in case after case, better services resulted, more quickly and over a broader geography, than either side of the partnership could have rendered up alone.

As a family of builders, the Fishers used physical facilities and infrastructure to get their foot in the door, as the starting point for arranging new solutions to unaddressed problems. But they never let the buildings become the end point. The buildings, produced with a speed and quality which would have taken years for public agencies to reproduce, were just the carrots. The Fishers recognized that the programs erected inside the shells were the most important element.

In this work, there was no doing without the Departments of Defense and Veterans Affairs, with their essential access to the relevant populations and highly skilled medical corps. But by staying in the driver's seat while creating new entities within public facilities, the Fishers used their valuable gifts to entice large government agencies to find creative ways to offer new services to Americans in need.

**PHYSICAL HEALTH,
MENTAL HEALTH**

Offering Rare Care with a Common Touch
Operation Mend's life-changing reconstructive surgery

Ronald Katz is an inventor and entrepreneur by profession, and though he never served in uniform, he now dedicates much of his energy and money to caring for members of the armed forces who were severely injured in the wars in Iraq and Afghanistan. Operation Mend, the program he started at the Ronald Reagan UCLA Medical Center, provides plastic and reconstructive surgery at no charge to those badly hurt in post-9/11 military service. In five years, Katz and other donors (like David Gelbaum's Iraq-Afghanistan Deployment Impact Fund, which donated a crucial $10 million to Operation Mend early on) have made possible hundreds of life-changing surgeries for more than 80 patients who were severely disfigured or burned—delivering immeasurable improvements in the quality of existence for these men and women.

Finding a Place among the Helpers

In 2004, Katz recalls, "I had decided that it was important for our family to contribute to the military serving in Iraq and Afghanistan. We really owe it to our military to support them." He met with officials at the Pentagon, discussed issues with experts, and considered endowing a fund for the children of servicemembers killed in action, until he learned that the Veterans Administration already provided a similar benefit.

After about a year of research, Katz met a senior military nurse who suggested that, given his interest in individuals, he consider visiting the San Antonio Military Medical Center (SAMMC) and supporting one of its Fisher Houses (comfort homes for families of servicemembers recovering at military medical centers—see case 8). "I went down there and was taken by the magnitude of suffering of those servicemembers who had been hurt," says Katz. His family quickly decided to become lead funders on one of the new Fisher Houses being built.

In 2006, Katz, his wife, Maddie, and his two sons flew down to SAMMC to attend the grand opening of two Fisher Houses and the Center for the Intrepid, a state-of-the-art physical rehabilitation center also constructed with private philanthropy.

> I vividly recall that there were about three or four thousand people at the opening and the first four rows of seating were roped off. I chuckled to my wife and my sons, "Boy, these must be for really important people." And sure enough, they were. They rolled in these men and women who were just catastrophically injured.

Though moved by the experience, Katz and his family were uncertain about their next step until a few months later when Ronald and Maddie were watching an interview with a severely burned Marine on CNN. "At the end," Katz recalls, "the interviewer said, 'Well, what's next for you?' And the Marine smiled with that burned smile and said, 'They gotta make me beautiful again.' And my wife was sitting next to me and she jabbed me in the ribs and said, 'Do something about this.'"

Sometimes Giving Takes Perseverance

As is often the case with the best philanthropy, the donor in this instance didn't just supply money (a $1 million founding gift), but also offered savvy guidance and linkage to important professional partners. Katz was already a board member at the Ronald Reagan UCLA Medical Center, so he approached the head of the medical school with an idea—he wanted to complement DoD and V.A. medical services by bringing catastrophically injured servicemembers to UCLA to receive plastic and reconstructive surgery from the university's world-class surgeons and facilities. Katz explained, "We'd like to make sure these men and women get the best this country has to offer, from both the public and the private sector." The head of the medical school gave his immediate support.

Along with UCLA surgeons Chris Crisera and Tim Miller, Katz visited SAMMC to pitch the idea to its commanding general. "I never realized the complexity of our offer," Katz admits. Although UCLA offered some of the very best surgeons and facilities at no cost, the partnership was not a traditional arrangement for the military. SAMMC's commanding general was responsible for every service member under his care, and referring patients with severe combat wounds to civilian medical facilities like UCLA was relatively uncharted territory.

Katz and the UCLA team worked to reassure SAMMC. Melanie Gideon, program manager at Operation Mend, recounts the conversations: "We will do everything we can to protect them from the moment they step off the plane. We will provide them with a buddy family in Los Angeles that will check on them if they need anything. They will be at a hotel right on campus. We will have someone accompany them to every appointment." Katz comments that "if you think of VIP treatments, we do VVIP treatments."

The commanding general at SAMMC sent one patient to start. Sure enough, it was the Marine the Katz family had seen on CNN months before. He had suffered burns on over a quarter of his body, as well as the loss of his ears, nose, and two fingers. Slowly but surely, over the course of dozens of surgeries, Operation Mend physicians replaced what he lost, crafting prosthetic ears and a nose, and grafting new skin to heal or replace scar tissue.

After observing the remarkable effects Operation Mend was having on patients, SAMMC slowly began sending more candidates. Many of them became prominent symbols of healing and recovery from the deepest depths of injury. "And so," as Katz puts it, "began the fabulous tale of Operation Mend."

The Core of the Work

Though founded and funded out of philanthropic generosity and a sense of

"We'd like to make sure these men and women get the best this country has to offer."
—Ronald Katz

moral obligation, Operation Mend functions as a strictly run medical practice tailored to a unique clientele. Says Gideon, "We know the responsibility we have to the military and our patients, and we take it very seriously."

First, Operation Mend aims to fill a niche, not duplicate services already provided by the Departments of Defense or Veterans Affairs. "We are a partner with the military," says Gideon. "We are not here to do something better than they are; we're not here to do something they already do. Our goal is to complement their services. Not every military medical center is armed with the top plastic surgeons in the world. That doesn't make sense for them, so we want to do our part."

By the end of its first year in 2008, SAMMC had sent Operation Mend six patients. Soon an official agreement was completed to cement the partnership. Operation Mend began receiving referrals from V.A. facilities, the Army Wounded Warrior Program, and the Marine Corps' Wounded Warrior Regiment.

Operation Mend also receives many of its patients by word of mouth. As Gideon explains, "If one guy is wounded in an IED blast, it generally means four of his friends were wounded in that same blast. One of them comes here, and he'll go tell his friends. Then we work backwards to get the approvals."

So what exactly does Operation Mend mend? Initially, the team focused solely on severe facial injuries caused primarily by burns. Because patients had often tried to put the flames out with their hands, the team soon expanded to include plastic and reconstructive surgery on hands. From there, they expanded to work on prosthetics, eye injuries, orthopedic problems, spinal damage, urogenital reconstruction, and even traumatic brain injury.

"We began to span our entire health system," says Gideon. But with each new possible patient procedure, the team goes back to the referring facility for authorization, to ensure their work doesn't interfere with that of the patient's military doctors.

Eligibility for Operation Mend requires that the service member be injured in post-9/11 combat or training; that the injury be one requiring unique care not available from local DoD or V.A. facilities; that a case manager from the referring institution serve as a local advocate for the patient; and that the patient travel with at least one other person. After the intake process, patients go to UCLA for an initial consultation and receive options for surgery or treatment. Patients then return home, schedule the surgery, and return for the procedure. During a surgery visit, patients will typically spend one night in the hospital immediately after the surgery and then one or two weeks in an on-campus hotel recovering before they travel home.

Operation Mend bills the patient's insurance, then covers whatever portion is not reimbursed. Gideon explains that "we realized that to establish a sustainable program where the doctor can continue to focus on these patients consistently," partial insurance payment was necessary. With Operation Mend's growth in size and patient load, professionalization was a must—"We now have 80 patients, 80 families, hundreds of surgeries, hundreds of nights of stay."

At the same time, the surgeons and other professionals who participate in Operation Mend do it because they believe in the program and its patients. They often change their practices, patient loads, and schedules to make Operation Mend patients a priority. "We have celebrities in the waiting room behind OpMend patients," says Gideon.

Cost varies by procedure, and includes transportation and lodging expenses for patient and family. Operation Mend has spent as little as $3,000 on a patient with a single clinical consultation, and over $500,000 on patients who have required more than 20 surgeries. Thanks to Operation Mend's host contributions and partial insurance reimbursements, it is able to provide life-changing care with reasonable philanthropic investment.

Gideon explains UCLA's role in keeping costs low. "We don't have to pay for physicians or nurses or anesthesiologists to come in from outside. They're all here. The volunteers are here. It's just a matter of getting all the moving parts together." The program's staff numbers only four—a program manager, clinical coordinator, and two assistant coordinators. Operation Mend benefits from sharing staff like a psychologist and finance manager with the university, and having access to the wider institution's marketing, media relations, and development resources.

While most patients have insurance through the military or Medicare Part B, Operation Mend will not turn patients away if they are uninsured. And it will never charge these severely wounded patients a dime for its services. The $1 million gift from the Katz family got the program off the ground, and another private donation of $10 million from the Iraq-Afghanistan Deployment Impact Fund helped sustain it.

Getting the Details Right

The magic of the program is not solely in the surgery provided. Katz's emphasis on the "VVIP treatment" seeps into every facet of Operation Mend, and makes its partnership with DoD and V.A. medical facilities work well. In order to provide the best care available, Operation Mend has "shifted from patient-centered care to family-centered care. We make sure that the whole puzzle is in one piece when patients leave," says Gideon. Operation Mend pays transportation, lodging, and per diem costs for patients and their families; it provides accompaniment to every appointment from arrival to departure; and it offers social and psychological support during often-difficult recovery periods.

Operation Mend brought on a psychologist from UCLA to work with patients and their families on care management, to conduct traumatic-stress assessments, and to help with the pressures of injury and surgical recovery. According to Gideon, some of the family members told the psychologist "this was the first time anyone has ever asked me what this has been like for me." In addition to immediate evaluation and counseling, Operation Mend has added a tele-health component to its treatment, so that patients and their families can get advice and counsel from UCLA professionals after returning home.

The needs of patients and their families often go beyond medical care, notes Katz. "They are here recovering for weeks after surgery—what are they going to do, sit in the hotel? So my son and daughter-in-law decided they wanted to start a Buddy Family program. The local family takes the patient out to dinner, to their home, to the beach, and many have developed a very close relationship with the individual and his family."

As more wounded men came to Operation Mend, more Buddy Families joined—there are currently 56 caring for 80 patients. Katz recently learned about "a 13-year-old boy who announced at his bar mitzvah that he was going to take the funds he received as presents and give them to Operation Mend. His family was a Buddy Family."

**PHYSICAL HEALTH,
MENTAL HEALTH, EDUCATION**

Investing
(and Investigating) Early
The Bob Woodruff Foundation

ABC News reporter Bob Woodruff left for Iraq in 2006 to embed as a reporter with American troops. While there, a roadside bomb exploded under his transport, leaving him with catastrophic injuries. Though he was a civilian, Woodruff was treated through the military-healthcare system because he sustained his injuries while covering the war effort. After spending 36 days in a coma, he began a lengthy recovery at Bethesda Naval Hospital.

It was here that Woodruff and his wife, Lee, found their motivation for the Bob Woodruff Foundation. "They realized the hospital was a special place as far as recuperation," says Barbara Lau, who directs charitable investments for the foundation. "The resiliency and the spirit they saw on the part of Bob's fellow patients inspired them." Bob and Lee Woodruff decided to channel the outpouring of financial support they were receiving from friends and business associates in television news into the Bob Woodruff Foundation, founded in 2007, with a focus on helping servicemembers who had been through experiences like Bob's.

The foundation soon found its niche in identifying at an initial stage promising investments on behalf of wounded post-9/11 servicemembers. Lau explains that "the Bob Woodruff Foundation doesn't make large grants." Instead it acts early to put a kind of philanthropic seal of approval on programs and organizations that appear to have a substantial upside.

The Bob Woodruff Foundation logged some initial wins by funding organizations like Student Veterans of America. SVA was just beginning when Woodruff gave it funding to hire a crucial staff member. The organization subsequently grew exponentially, and currently has active independent chapters on several hundred campuses. (See case 5 for details.)

Tens of thousands of nonprofits list veterans as one of their primary client populations, a number that increased tenfold in the past decade. There is lots of chaff mixed in with the grains of wheat. As an early actor in veterans philanthropy, the foundation has gone through a learning curve. "There are organizations we have funded in the past that we would not fund again today," admits Lau.

Moreover, a dizzying array of new *types* of services is now being offered to veterans, servicemembers, and families—everything from art therapy to service dogs to adaptive sports. Many of these are not new, but their application to the military world is, and how useful they will be remains to be seen. So how can an experimental foundation identify promising openings in a field as young, broad, unconsolidated, and unproven as much of today's philanthropy for veterans is?

One technique the Woodruff Foundation has used is to convene groups of operators and force them to hash out definitions and goals and criteria in new fields. For example, in 2011, the foundation received funding applications for several programs anxious to cycle veterans into perspective-changing "adaptive-sports" programs (which pull people with disabilities into activities like skiing, kayaking, cycling, hiking, etc.). After some research, Lau felt she didn't know enough about the value of such activity to offer funding. Yet the potential seemed real.

So the Woodruff Foundation invited several dozen service providers, along with experts from the Department of Veterans Affairs, to explore the field's possibilities. "The motivation was simply to learn what comprises a good adaptive sports program. So we got all these people together in a room," Lau explains.

Over two days, for a relatively modest price tag of $40,000, attendees met in small groups to "talk about best practices, what really works, the actual number of people participating in these programs, versus the perceived wisdom that everybody bandies around." Conclusions were compiled and "now we have a set of criteria that we can use in making decisions on which adaptive-sports programs we're going to fund."

The findings were also distributed to attendees and other interested parties, establishing for the first time a set of guidelines for adaptive-sports programs aimed at veterans. "The goal was to educate ourselves. But in the process we can also educate others," says Lau.

A V.A. official attending the adaptive sports conference was so impressed he remarked, "Well, I had my PowerPoint and prepared remarks, but I'm throwing them out the window because we, the V.A., have learned so much in the past two days that we're going to go back and fix some things." Lau's philosophy is that if a philanthropy can "get good people in a room together, then add some structure, guidance, and creativity, lots of good things can happen."

How many other segments of veterans philanthropy might benefit from such gatherings of experts? Woodruff plans to stage one similar conference per quarter for the near future, on topics ranging from employment to art therapy to peer-to-peer mentoring to the use of service dogs for PTSD. Where only a few years ago, many funders would be forced to make a best guess as to which programs showed promise, the Woodruff Foundation is working to consolidate judgments to avoid mistakes and wasted effort.

When It's Time to Ask for Something Fresh

As mentioned, Student Veterans of America benefitted from some savvy early giving by the Woodruff Foundation. After the foundation's funding for staff helped SVA take off, the donor and service provider gradually entered into a continuing "open conversation." Lau explains that "as part of our funding process we do so much research and talk to so many people, very often the questions we ask can spark some new thinking and direction."

So eventually when SVA asked the Woodruff Foundation for continued staff funding, the foundation declined. But learning that SVA was planning a

> A dizzying array of services is being offered to veterans. How can a foundation identify promising openings in a field as unconsolidated at this?

program to train students as peer mentors on mental-health issues, Woodruff jumped at the chance to support the work. Student Veterans of America had already partnered with the University of Michigan on a program to train upperclassmen at 10 SVA chapters to function as "mental health gatekeepers." The university taught them to recognize depression and other problems, and to refer students to counseling resources.

On receiving Woodruff's encouragement, SVA and the University of Michigan geared up to expand the program. The foundation was an enthusiastic supporter. In Lau's words, "Vets like to talk to other vets—yes, that's true—so, let's develop that in a structured way and give peer mentors the training they need to be successful." Thus, what might have ended as a failed grant application in other places turned into a successful program enhancement.

MENTAL HEALTH

Building a Sense of Purpose
The Mission Continues exercises the leadership skills of vets

One of the ways new ideas spread is through their association with charismatic public figures. Habitat for Humanity first took off as an organization when, in 1984, former President Jimmy Carter volunteered to help out on one of its building projects. Eric Greitens, founder of the Mission Continues, has the sort of personal star power which has already begun to attract public and financial support for his new approach to helping veterans of the wars in Iraq and Afghanistan adjust to post-military life. Greitens is a former Navy SEAL and a former Rhodes Scholar.

He argues that the recent focus on treating veterans primarily as victims—whether of post-traumatic stress disorder or other maladies—may be not only expensive but counter-productive for the intended beneficiary. While, to be sure, veterans with severe psychological or medical problems need the clinical treatment they've been promised through the $136 billion-plus annual federal budget appropriation for the Department of Veterans Affairs, it's Greitens' view that these entitlements almost inevitably fail to address the deeper need of veterans seeking to build new lives: a sense of purpose.

Many Americans enter the military in the first place out of a desire to protect, to work in cooperative teams, to contribute to their nation, to serve a deeper cause than simple self-interest. "It is crucial," says Greitens, "that veterans have the opportunity to satisfy their desire to serve." The key to supporting many veterans, he says, is finding ways for them to continue to lead and help others—to extend "their mission of public service."

The same impulse which brought these men and women to military service can thus power their new lives. Greitens is not shy about casting this as fundamentally different from the approach that many veterans' lobbies and government agencies take. His alternative is based on the idea that "a veteran can build a successful transition not on things—benefits that they've been given—but on skills, and their desire to help."

Tapping the Hunger to Serve a Purpose

In 2007, Greitens embodied his idea in a new organization. After returning from a deployment to Iraq, he used his combat pay to found the Mission Continues. The organization is different right from the beginning: its two-week orientation begins with a mass swearing-in. Once they are trained, participants begin their new "missions" with established public-service organizations—Big Brothers Big Sisters, Mothers Against Drunk Driving, Habitat for Humanity, the Boys and Girls Clubs, the Red Cross, or a wide range of other national and local nonprofits.

Participants are called "fellows," and they receive modest stipends drawn from the group's annual $6 million budget to support them as they serve at least 24 hours every week, for 26 weeks. Most of the Fellows, though not all, have been designated as disabled by the Department of Veterans Affairs. In effect, the Mission Continues assists these veterans by focusing them less on their problems than on their value to others, providing them with a path toward what Greitens calls "a renewed sense of purpose."

Many participants subsequently return to school, start their own businesses, or become staff members at the organizations where they served their fellowship. A study conducted by the school of social work at Washington University tracked 52 alumni who completed the fellowship program between 2007 and 2010 and found that "71 percent had gone on to further their education and 86 percent have transferred their skills to civilian employment."

More subjectively, the study found that "the majority of participants report that the fellowship helped them to become leaders within their communities (86 percent), and to teach others the value of service, and to sustain a role for service within their communities (91 percent)." Notably, some 64 percent of the fellows, almost all Iraq- and Afghanistan-era veterans, had been classified as suffering from post-traumatic stress disorder. The Mission Continues, in other words, is taking on plenty of hard cases, and producing good results with them.

Bridging the Military-civilian Divide

Greitens' mission goes beyond helping individual veterans. He also aims to change the public view of the 300,000 veterans who will be leaving the military in the coming three to five years from that of victims with special needs to

> Entitlements for veterans almost inevitably fail to address the deeper need of former servicemembers seeking to build new lives— which is a sense of purpose.

one of "citizen leaders." Toward that end, the Mission Continues fellows, staff, and volunteer recruiters help to lead large-scale nationwide "service days," whose projects bring veterans together with legions of Americans who might otherwise never have contact with any of the 1 percent of their fellow citizens who serve in the military.

Recent service days saw veteran-led volunteers distribute supplies and help clean up in areas of New York City ravaged by Hurricane Sandy, while another group renovated a 4-H center in Bexar, Texas, where service dogs are trained. Fellows of the Mission Continues literally become squad leaders again, managing dozens of local volunteers in day-long and multi-day efforts. In the process, veterans make new friends and contacts, and everyday Americans view former military members in an entirely new light.

Service-day projects also link veterans directly with employees from many of the major corporations who provide most of the financial support for the

Mission Continues. Goldman Sachs and Goldman Sachs Gives, the charitable arm of the bank, have pledged $6 million to support the group's fellowship program. The Home Depot Foundation donated $1.05 million to the organization in the latest year, and Home Depot employees joined forces with the Mission Continues on more than 300 community-service projects. Target has given $750,000 to the group in recent years, and the company's employees have worked side-by-side with Fellows on many service projects. Additional supporters have included the Draper Richards Kaplan Foundation, the New Profit venture philanthropy fund, Novo Nordisk, JPMorgan Chase, Southwest Airlines, the Hauck Foundation, the Bob Woodruff Foundation, the Paul E. Singer Foundation and others.

With this support, the Mission Continues grew substantially during its first five years of existence. It started as a small local program in St. Louis. Today the organization has three offices, in St. Louis, Houston, and New York, from which it serves veterans in 43 states.

Defining Success as Many Local Achievements

Greitens is clearly interested in influencing America's culture beyond the number of individuals touched directly by the Mission Continues. And he doesn't judge achievement by how large his own program becomes. "Our measure of success is not to have one giant Mission Continues with 200,000 fellowships," he says pointedly. He would be just as happy to inspire and influence others to start parallel programs, and he is actively working toward that end.

"We hope to have a high-impact, well-run nonprofit that produces outstanding results." And he would be happy to be copied, "all over the country, in ways that make sense for individual communities." One approach he's now trying: to convince major national nonprofits, including Big Brothers Big Sisters and Habitat for Humanity, to incorporate a fellowship program for veterans right inside their hundreds of chapters. Changing the way America sees its veterans is the mission, and Greitens' own group is just one instrument deployed toward that end.

(researched by Howard Husock)

MENTAL HEALTH

Tapping the Power of *Pro Bono*

Case and Eli Lilly spread Give an Hour across the nation

In 2005, Barbara Van Dahlen was a successful child psychologist in Bethesda, Maryland. "I loved it," she says, "but had a feeling I could probably take what I knew and apply it on a bigger scale to help more people." During her training years earlier, Van Dahlen had encountered Vietnam veterans in mental-health centers. With all we've learned since then, she thought, surely the nation will be prepared for the psychological needs of those coming home from Iraq and Afghanistan.

After hearing news stories about returning veterans adjusting to civilian life, Van Dahlen decided that rather than just observing the process she might become a helpful contributor. Her solution was simple, and had deep professional roots: "Most of us in this field are encouraged to do *pro bono* work. I thought: I'd be willing to give a little bit of my time, build it into my practice."

Why not donate some of her expertise every week, and ask professional colleagues to do likewise? Taken together, their individual contributions could amount to quite a substantial resource. With a little naming advice from her daughter, she founded Give an Hour (GAH).

Van Dahlen not only had a full-time weekly caseload of 28 to 30 patients, but also managed two offices and a team of associates. And she had daughters to raise. Yet Van Dahlen had always considered service to others as central to her life's work. By the time she had the idea for GAH, she had already been volunteering her time for years, and loved donating her services to low-income families. "I assumed that there must be other clinicians out there like me who, seeing a need, would want to provide care. And if I made it easy for them to give, they would."

Van Dahlen realized that if she could involve some of her fellow psychologists, counselors, and psychiatrists, her volunteer efforts could be repeated many times over, and many more veterans could be helped. That might well have ended as a private pipe dream. Van Dahlen had no background in managing charitable work. She had no funds to set up a network capable of matching veterans looking for guidance with professionals willing to donate their services.

Fortunately for the thousands of men and women who have since benefited from the services donated by Give an Hour, the Case Foundation of Washington, D.C., stepped in to help build a framework for spreading its volunteer mental-health services far and wide. "We invest in people and ideas that can change the world," says Jean Case, who started the foundation with her husband, Steve, the co-founder of internet pioneer AOL. "Where something transformative has happened, there's usually a great leader behind it," she notes.

Case had known Van Dahlen and admired her organizing energy before Give an Hour was even dreamed up. "Barbara started with an idea, but she really needed to turn that into a concrete plan and begin to assemble a team. We are a foundation that is comfortable with that early stage of investment. We don't just write checks; we surround organizations with resources and support in every way, connect them to people, and bring talent."

Case saw promise in the idea of getting lots of professionals to each give a little. During her time as chair of the President's Council on Service and civic Participation, she had previously recruited large corporations to donate *pro bono* help to nonprofits in certain high-skill areas like accounting and marketing. The Case Foundation didn't become financial supporters of Give an Hour until several years into their relationship, but Jean Case made valuable introductions, especially on the organizational and computer technology fronts, that allowed Van Dahlen to gradually build her young nonprofit into a working national exemplar.

Getting mental-health professionals to donate an hour of time per week seemed plausible. The "risk in the business model," as Case puts it, lay in matching them to veterans in their area. "How do we connect them with people in need?" asked Van Dahlen.

Their answer was an internet platform. Inspired by Craigslist, the informal online market for goods and services, they built a simple matching service. "If we can create something where we've got the providers on one side, and those in need have access to them, bingo," thought Van Dahlen. She recruited a team that used open-source technology to build an online mechanism for matching veterans wanting help with mental-health volunteers in their area.

The seeker simply puts in his zip code and how many miles he is willing to travel. He can request general counseling, or zero in on any number of special areas (marriage counseling, child therapy, substance-abuse help, bereavement services, brain injuries, anger management, pastoral guidance, and others). He can make an appointment in an office or request telephone counseling. Providers are available in a wide range of health specialties, and both veterans and any of their household members are eligible for the free services.

When the volunteer providers register, Give an Hour confirms their identities, verifies their licenses, and checks for any problems in their professional records before allowing patients to contact them. If a patient has difficulty finding a convenient or properly specialized provider, Give an Hour works with him to find a professional he can consult by phone, or tries to recruit a new provider in an area where none exists.

"Even in places like Texas where we have hundreds of providers, we occasionally have niches where someone might have to drive an hour and a half to the closest volunteer," says GAH program specialist Jess Grove. Grove manages the provider network, and arranges about 50 "warm handoffs" per month on average.

When she was recruiting volunteer professionals, one of Van Dahlen's crucial early partners was Paul Burke, president of the American Psychiatric Foundation, the charitable arm of the American Psychiatric Association. When the two met, Burke was impressed with Van Dahlen's "crystal-clear image. I was struck by the simplicity of the call to action: Just give an hour of your time, whether you are a psychiatrist, a psychologist, a social worker.

> *"I thought: I'd be willing to donate some of my time. Why not ask professional colleagues to do likewise?"*
>
> —Barbara Van Dahlen

I didn't see anyone else doing that in an organized way." With more than 25,000 member psychiatrists, the APA served as an ideal recruiting pool for Van Dahlen's burgeoning army of mental-health donors. Within a year, the first 500 *pro bono* professionals were signed up.

The Eli Lilly and Company Foundation Takes a Chance

Give an Hour's partnership with the American Psychiatric Foundation went beyond recruiting volunteers. The two organizations won a $1 million grant from the Eli Lilly and Company Foundation (Lilly Foundation). The money was provided to allow the two groups to conduct a national public awareness campaign, and help Give an Hour connect veterans to professionals.

As a major pharmaceutical firm, Eli Lilly has both deep expertise in mental health and a finger on the pulse of the medical community. In 2007, Lilly Foundation president Rob Smith recognized an opening for philanthropy—the burdens of war, including mental-health strains, fell on a small fraction of the population, and although many health-care providers wanted to contribute to the well-being of the military population, few had any available outlet.

A Lilly Foundation associate brought Van Dahlen's work to Smith's attention. "It was a great match with what we had been looking for—a systematic way to tap into talented people and give them an opportunity to give something back to help our soldiers and their families." A major investment in a brand-new 501(c)(3) charity was, however, unheard of at the foundation at that time. Its two big philanthropic projects were five-year $30 million grants to well-established organizations combating diabetes and drug-resistant tuberculosis.

As a young organization, Give an Hour would be a risk. Smith received many questions from his board and colleagues. Yet "the more I interacted with Barbara, the greater confidence I had that this was not only a good idea, but that she had the skills and connections and credibility to pull it off," he explains.

The Lilly Foundation played an important role in funding and counseling Give an Hour through the tricky process of "building supply and demand at generally the same time." If the group had expanded its provider database without reaching out to potential clients at the same time, the mental-health professionals might have become disillusioned at not being engaged quickly enough. If client demand had been built up without sufficient providers, Give an Hour would have been in the terrible position of making promises on which it could not deliver. Yet keeping these two elements in balance was not easy.

With its three-year seven-figure grant from the Lilly Foundation, Give an Hour went to work. The partnership with the American Psychiatric Foundation led to alliance with more than a dozen associations of mental-health professionals, like the National Association of Social Workers and the American Psychological Association. Give an Hour was able to increase the size of its *pro bono* network from about 1,000 providers in 2008 to more than 6,500 in 2012, with representation in all 50 states. The cumulative number of counseling hours donated since founding increased from 1,400 in 2008 to more than 82,000 hours by the fourth quarter of 2012.

> Give an Hour's platform on the Internet allows patients to get services easily while maintaining personal privacy.

On the client side, Give an Hour used television and radio spots to mount a public education and awareness campaign. Around $2.5 million in donated media time was secured. Messages were ultimately aired on 300 television channels and 750 radio stations.

The Give an Hour model has two major strengths. It makes things simple for mental-health professionals to volunteer their time. And its open platform allows patients to easily get services without stigma, or approval from insurance or a physician, while maintaining personal privacy.

These same strengths, however, also make it hard to evaluate the program methodically. While each mental-health professional is responsible for tracking and treating Give an Hour patients just like any others in their individual practices, no patient data makes its way back to the national organization. Thus, official outcome assessments aren't possible.

"I got a lot of pressure to have patients register with the national Give an Hour headquarters. But I said no—it has to be confidential and anonymous," explains Van Dahlen about her hard choice. The relationship between individual patients and individual volunteers is direct and unmediated. The number of *pro bono* hours given is therefore how the organization measures its impact.

Beyond Matching Patients and Providers

In addition to its core mission of convincing mental-health professionals to donate an hour per week to veterans in a traditional clinical capacity, Give an Hour has also taken on some additional contributions. The group cooperates with the Wounded Warrior Project, a nonprofit that, among other programs, runs a call-in center for veterans. WWP refers its callers in need of mental-health services to Give an Hour, and Give an Hour trains and provides medical personnel as group counselors on WWP recovery trips.

Give an Hour has also provided mental-health volunteers to assist Team Rubicon, a service organization that uses veterans as first-responders after natural disasters. Van Dahlen's group has also helped fellow nonprofit Student Veterans of America bring a mental-health lens to their work with veterans on college campuses. Give an Hour has also embarked on a project to offer 100,000 mental-health providers with specific training that will make them more effective with patients who have military backgrounds.

Early on, Van Dahlen received many questions about how her work meshed with what the Department of Defense and Department of Veterans Affairs were supposed to provide. Her answer? "We're here to fill gaps—there are phenomenal clinicians at the V.A. and DoD, but they can't be everywhere at once." It's not only geographic and convenience issues that make Give an Hour attractive for many individuals; there are also eligibility issues. Family members, for instance, often don't qualify for public benefits, but Give an Hour is happy to counsel all.

Interestingly, government agencies have begun to approach Give an Hour about working together. Van Dahlen reports that in late 2012, "the Army National Guard reached out to me and said, 'We have a problem—we have nowhere to refer some of the women and men who have experienced sexual trauma.'" With a memorandum of understanding in place, the National Guard now refers those whom it can't help to Give an Hour's network of providers. Similarly, the nonprofit now has a memorandum of agreement with the V.A. by which suicide coordinators can refer certain patients to Give an Hour for services.

In just the few years since its founding, the increases in *pro bono* time offered and taken up through Give an Hour have been impressive. From just 2010 to the end of 2012, *pro bono* hours jumped 25-fold. A conservative estimate of the value of the time contributed by its mental-health volunteers is $8.3 million since the group's founding. It costs the national organization $17 per hour donated to maintain and build the network and provide these services to clients at no charge.

MENTAL HEALTH

Remaking Mental-health Care
The Dallas Foundation fills a gap fast with a nonprofit neighbor

When David Gelbaum offered his $243 million gift to aid current and former military members during the height of the Iraq war (see case 1), getting the funds to groups that could use them fast enough to have immediate impact was a challenge. To involve local experts in targeting grants, Gelbaum's Iraq-Afghanistan Deployment Impact Fund placed large sums in the hands of community foundations in states like Texas and Florida, with instructions to re-grant the money to particular groups in their states doing good work. In this way, the

Dallas Foundation became a conduit for distributing millions of dollars of IADIF money over a period of five years.

Among other achievements, $1.2 million in Dallas Foundation funds seed-ed a novel mental-health program at a nonprofit hospital near Fort Hood in Killeen, Texas. Thanks to these independent philanthropic resources, Scott & White Hospital has been able to sidestep government bureaucracy and offer nonprofit mental-health services that would otherwise have been unavail-able to many of the recipients. More than 28,000 soldiers and military family members have benefited from high-quality confidential treatment as a result.

Sometimes an Outside Institution Can Be Better

When the Dallas Foundation and two other Texas community foundations received money from IADIF to redistribute, the first thing they did was to commission a survey to determine areas of greatest need. In less than two months, they had a list of seven funding priorities. In early 2007, when needs assessments were scant, this information provided the foundations with a use-ful guide by which to judge proposals.

Mental health was one of the issues that Laura Ward of the Dallas Foun-dation hoped to address early on. She was concerned, though, that issues of stigma and trust might complicate delivery of services to soldiers and their families. "We knew that getting people to come was a problem," says Ward. When Scott & White Hospital applied for a grant, however, she thought she might be looking at a solution.

Killeen, Texas, a town of about 55,000, has two major assets—Fort Hood (then home to two full divisions of soldiers), and a Scott & White Hospital (part of a major nonprofit medical network that has served central Texas for more than a century). Matthew Wright, a vice president at Scott & White, notes that Fort Hood functioned as one of the U.S. military's foremost gateways to the Middle East over the last decade. "There were some wise commanders on Fort Hood around 2006–2007 who realized the uptick in deployments to Iraq and Afghanistan was going to inundate the official military mental-health capacity. They said, 'We need to reach out to our surrounding community and ask for help.'"

As war-zone rotations of locally based soldiers ramped up, a retired three-star general living in Killeen named Don Jones approached the com-mander of the Fort Hood medical center and asked what he could do to help. According to Jones, the commander responded, "Well, we have two mental-health workers here for two divisions of soldiers." Luckily Jones had some experience in this area, including a stint after leaving the military helping the American Red Cross implement its mental-health program in disaster response.

Jones suggested that rather than inventing something new they take advantage of their proximity to the Scott & White Hospital. While the base and the hospital had worked together before—they were, after all, the area's two largest employers—they had never collaborated on a project as sensitive as mental-health services. A short time after the leadership at Fort Hood approached Scott & White, Maxine Trent joined the hospital to run the new program. She was a perfect match—in addition to being a family-therapy clinician, she was an Army child herself, and a Navy spouse.

By 2008, families at Fort Hood were going through their second and third deployments to Iraq and Afghanistan. Families were "getting barely enough time to catch their breath, and then going through another deployment," explains Trent. The combination of combat stress and family reset issues created plenty of demand for services.

There were, however, cultural, professional, and financial barriers that discouraged resort to mental-health care. "Soldiers were not seeking help, over concern of what the impact would be on their military careers," says Jones. "I even found soldiers in Fort Hood who were driving to Austin, Texas, to get mental-health counseling at their own expense."

Although the Defense Department has recently put extensive effort into decreasing the stigma surrounding mental health, Scott & White realized it faced an uphill battle to overcome the perceived weakness of seeking treatment. To build credibility, the hospital hired therapists who were ex-military or military dependents. "The military ID card and a former rank go a long way in terms of trust," explains Wright. "And then word of mouth took over."

The hospital also never labeled its offices as "mental-health clinics." Instead it co-located those services with its pediatric and adult primary-care clinics, so that no individual had to identify as a mental-health patient. Using the primary-care clinics with which many Fort Hood families were already familiar also put patients at ease.

Ward and the Dallas Foundation were impressed by the way Scott & White got around the issue of stigma. "They created a way for people to visit, and taught their physicians to recognize stress symptoms and plug patients right away into mental-health services without it ever touching their record. They already had a captive audience that trusted their hospital."

Working hard to balance cooperation with the Army with independence on behalf of patients, Trent earned the trust of leaders at Fort Hood. She understood the military well enough to know that commanding officers are responsible for all aspects of the lives under their command, and that ceding some of that to an outside organization is a risk. The response was to "set up the right channels for sharing critical information." In situations where patients posed a threat to themselves or others, base leadership would be involved. Otherwise, the Army would not have access to details of those seeking help at the hospital. Once comfort was established, the Army medical center began referring patients to the hospital, and hospital staff were allowed to visit Family Readiness Groups and other support organizations on base to spread word about their services.

Restructuring Medical Care through Philanthropy

The stigma sometimes attached to mental-health services can make for difficulty not only in seeking help, but in paying for it as well. Sometimes, says Matthew Wright of Scott & White, "the obstacle to mental-health treatment is the diagnostic code. It will determine whether or not insurance will pay for the procedure." Sometimes a person feels stuck between a rock and a hard place. "If I'm under stress and need someone to talk to, and I self-pay, there's not a problem. But most of us can't do that. If I have a diagnostic code that allows insurance to pay for it, that means it goes on my service record and I get diagnosed with a problem."

How does Scott & White get around this dilemma? Via philanthropy. "If we use philanthropy to pay for it, the only thing we need to keep track of is the patient count, and measurements of success," says Wright.

The hospital takes inventories before and after counseling to measure success. "If what the patient wants is relief from hyper-vigilance, then we use clinical measures to assess your hyper-vigilance on the first session, on the third session, on the sixth session," explains Trent. "We use treatments supported by clinical data, and we compare our progress to that. So we're measuring our interventions the whole time."

Relying on philanthropy rather than insurance or self-pay also frees the hospital to run the program very flexibly. For instance, instead of paying its therapists per patient-hour of treatment, as most clinics do, the grants from the Dallas Foundation and other donors allowed Scott

"We have two mental-health workers here for two divisions of soldiers," said the commander. Philanthropy filled the gap.

& White to pay therapists a salary. Then they "see as many people as they ethically and clinically can. If this person needs 15 minutes, give them 15 minutes. The next person who comes in may need an hour and a half; give them an hour and a half," say Wright. By changing the economic model, philanthropy allowed a given amount of dollars to go further and treat patients more effectively.

The results were stunning. The hospital expected to see 900 patients in their first 18 months; instead it treated 1,800 patients in the first *four* months. In 2009, when a disturbed Islamist serving at Fort Hood killed 13 people and wounded many more, the hospital was there to provide support, providing over 600 appointments to those affected by the event. Thanks to timely philanthropy, Scott & White helped a total of more than 28,000 patients during the period when deployment stress was most severe at one of America's largest military bases.

MENTAL HEALTH

Spreading Good Ideas in Mental Health

The McCormick Foundation and Welcome Back Veterans

In 1955, Col. Robert McCormick, owner and publisher of the *Chicago Tribune* and a decorated military officer and veteran of World War I, passed away, leaving in his will instructions for the creation of a charitable trust devoted to public purposes. The foundation made large contributions to military causes during the 1950s and '60s through its creation of the First Division Museum, a very fine historical facility and military research archive in Wheaton, Illinois.

The grantmaking of the McCormick Foundation took a renewed shift toward the needs of veterans, servicemembers, and their families in the later 2000s. McCormick operates a "Communities Program," which matches funds donated by the public fifty cents to the dollar, and then uses the foundation's significant grantmaking expertise to help the fund make savvy charitable investments. In 2008, a group of Chicago investors opened a fund under the program to support Operation Healing Freedom. This supported a treatment institute for mild brain injuries, a rehabilitation center for wounded servicemembers, comfort homes for family members nursing servicemembers, local employment programs, and scholarships for veterans.

Operation Healing Freedom caught the attention of Fred Wilpon, majority owner of the New York Mets baseball team. He proposed setting up a similar partnership between McCormick and Major League Baseball to fund veterans programs around the country. It was called Welcome Back Veterans. The fund's first two rounds of donations were broad in scope and geography, but in 2010 McCormick sharpened its focus. "Based on what we learned, we zeroed in on mental-health services at major medical centers," explains Anna Laubach, director of veterans' initiatives for McCormick.

The Red Sox Lead the League in Mental-health Services

After winning the World Series in 2007, the Boston Red Sox players and ownership team took a trip to Washington, D.C., for a White House ceremony. During the visit, Larry Ronan, the team's medical director and a passionate disaster-response physician with connections to the military, organized a tour of the Walter Reed Army Medical Center for the players. Shortly after, the team's charitable arm, the Red Sox Foundation, approached Massachusetts General Hospital, one of the nation's leading psychiatric-health centers with more than 600 faculty members, to propose a partnership for assisting veterans. Opening its doors in 2010, the program provides mental-health care (treating about 500 New England veterans in its first two years), trains professionals on military trauma, and conducts research on traumatic stress and brain injuries.

The McCormick Foundation saw the potential for bringing this program to other medical centers around the country. The foundation provided $2.9 million to match funds raised by Major League Baseball, then added another $2.2 million a year later. Programs similar to the one at Mass General sprang up in Atlanta, as a partnership between Emory University Medical Center and the Atlanta Braves baseball team, and at UCLA, Stanford, Weill-Cornell, University of Michigan, Rush University, and Duke medical centers. To date,

> The goal is to make the whole of veterans services greater than the sum of the disconnected parts.

the McCormick Foundation and Major League Baseball have committed a combined $30 million toward these projects.

Welcome Back Veterans not only provides excellent clinical services to its clients, but also allows high-caliber medical centers to share research and promising practices. "We get together once per quarter. The clinicians are hungry to work together, and learn from other programs that are slightly different from theirs," reports Michael Allard, the program's chief at Massachusetts General Hospital.

Among the great successes of Welcome Back Veterans is its 14-part training series for clinicians, created in collaboration with the Department of Veterans Affairs' National Center on PTSD. Participants take a pre-test, go through the educational program, take an evaluation after training, and a three-month follow-up survey to measure how much they've improved their military cultural competence. Welcome Back Veterans expected a few hundred participants to enroll; instead, it has trained more than 5,700 and growing. Through its investment in Welcome Back Veterans, McCormick has thus supported not only treatment at the network's medical centers, but also a collective improvement in the environment of mental-health care for veterans and their families.

In 2008, the foundation's 10-year strategic plan promised to help veterans by supporting what it calls "systems of care." Rather than singling out individual issues such as employment, mental health, or education, McCormick sees its best opportunities in bringing order and coordination to private and public resources that already exist. The goal is to make the whole of veterans services greater than the sum of the disconnected parts.

MENTAL HEALTH

Clinical Philanthropists
Bristol-Myers Squibb shows how to measure results

When people say, "There's so much out there and we don't really know what works," our response is, "that's one of the funder's responsibilities to facilitate."

—John Damonti, president,
Bristol-Myers Squibb Foundation

In 2010, the Bristol-Myers Squibb Foundation (BMSF), the philanthropic arm of the bio-pharmaceutical company, had no history of giving to veterans, servicemembers, or their families. By the end of 2012, it had committed nearly $7 million to such projects—ranging from evaluating web-based mental-health interventions for veterans who would not seek treatment through traditional avenues, to a new model of community-based support for military populations. And thanks to a clear investment strategy and the scientific culture of its corporate parent, BMSF's early giving in this field has already attracted major public and private funders to support the work it is piloting and evaluating.

While BMSF remains a relative newcomer to this branch of philanthropy, it benefits from a funding strategy honed over the last 15 years. Established in 1955, the foundation aims to reduce health disparities by strengthening the capacity of healthcare workers, integrating medical care with support services, and mobilizing communities in the fight against disease. The company focuses on developing medicines to treat unmet medical needs, while the foundation focuses on the role communities can play to improve health outcomes. Using as an example HIV/AIDS in Africa (one of the foundation's program areas), BMSF president John Damonti explains that "you could have all the medication you need to control the virus, but at the end of the day, if you don't have the right nutritional supplementation, if you haven't disclosed to your partner, if stigma is high, you're not likely to get maximal benefit."

BMSF taps its core business for skills and technical guidance on grantmaking. "On our foundation board, we've got our heads of medical and regulatory affairs, as well as the heads of our global businesses—they're always pushing us to take the same approach with our grants as they do with their business," says foundation director Catharine Grimes. "We look for more than just goals and objectives. We try to evaluate grants through a clinical-trial approach," explains Grimes. The foundation often advises that grantees bring on independent evaluators to implement objective assessments.

Grantees are sometimes surprised at the centrality of evaluation in BMSF's giving, says Grimes, and "will ask, 'Really, there's budget for that?' Our answer is that it's absolutely necessary—you can't afford not to do it." The foundation homes in on one particular type of evaluation: program efficacy. "A lot of funders focus on *outputs*—how many patients go through this," explains Grimes. "But we're focused on hard data on the health *outcomes*."

A New Venture into Military Philanthropy
When Grimes left her position in the company's neuroscience depart-

ment and joined the foundation in mid-2010, she inherited a portfolio of mental-health programs focused primarily on populations with severe mental illnesses. Not finding many avenues for piloting new approaches, only replication and expansion, Grimes decided to turn her attention to serving new populations.

Tipped off by a friend exiting the military, Grimes saw great potential for BMSF in helping veterans who needed help settling into new civilian lives. "It was a place where we could build out a strong grant program according to our strategy—modeling supportive community services." The move was met with wholehearted support from the foundation board and the company itself (which simultaneously created a Veterans Community Network, a group of 500 employees committed to recruiting and retaining veterans within the company). Very quickly, the veterans mental-health program at the foundation became one of the most popular recipients of donations from the employee-giving campaign. Damonti explains that company employees "feel good about our work with AIDS in Africa, they feel good about our work on oncology in Central and Eastern Europe, they feel good about our work on hepatitis in Asia, but there's this whole other layer of passion around mental health among veterans."

Passion alone, however, does not make effective philanthropy. Grimes freely admits, "We didn't know the space—we were new. But what we did know, and I think this is where a lot of funders weren't as clear, is what kind of grants we were looking to make. We have a very clear strategy for our grantmaking, so we know what kinds of proposals fit into our wheelhouse and what kinds don't." Their strategy was clear—pilot and rigorously evaluate new models of community-support services in mental health for veterans, servicemembers, and their families.

To fill the still-sizable gap between clear guidelines and concrete grants, Grimes turned BMSF's lack of experience into an advantage—they encouraged grantees to come up with new ideas to test. Grimes explains:

> We posted an open call for concepts on our website. Three pages—it wasn't even a full proposal. I just wanted ideas, and left it very open-ended. We got about 80 replies to that in 2011 and 150 in 2012. We could wade through the stack quickly because we had this clear focus on community-based care. But then you get down to 25 to 35 that are really innovative and interesting models. Both years, we invited full proposals on 15.

From those full proposals, BMSF whittled the options down based on available funds at the foundation, the program's focus on unmet needs, and the applicant's evaluation plan. Twelve grants were made, most of them lasting two to three years. Between continuing and new project funding, BMSF's annual budget for this portfolio hovers around $4 million.

Testing Mental Health Interventions

In its 2012 grant cycle, BMSF used its prowess in clinical evaluation to bridge the gap between an innovation of private philanthropy and the funding requirements of the Department of Veterans Affairs. Grimes learned about a program called VetsPrevail that delivers personalized early mental-health interventions over the internet to patients who would not seek traditional treatment. The program had received funding from several private foundations and the National Science Foundation. Its results seemed promising, yet the V.A. was unable to fund the program because no rigorous evaluation existed for it.

> The Bristol-Myers Squibb Foundation taps its core business for skills and technical guidance on grantmaking.

Perplexed, Grimes asked, "It's got a lot of big funders. Do you mean they didn't engage in an evaluation of the program?" She investigated and found that the private funders and the V.A. were defining "evaluation" differently. For the private foundations, evaluations delineated goals and targets in terms of patients served, rather than outcomes achieved. "This," Grimes reflects, "is when I started learning what a different approach we have from other funders." Grimes knew that what was really needed was "documentation of the program's efficacy. As a science foundation running a mental-health program, we understand that."

So BMSF brought on Rush University to develop a research protocol and determine whether VetsPrevail actually reduces the symptoms it targets. Just as important, Grimes brought on "a steering committee of V.A. members to make sure that the design met their criteria and that if they found positive efficacy, it is something they would look to implement in their facilities." BMSF made sure to include a range of medical professionals, research scientists, program officers, and even technology experts who might eventually be responsible for implementing the program.

Damonti explains the design: "The evaluation is enrolling 150 vets who will get the VetsPrevail intervention, and 150 subjects who will not, and comparing them. This is what our company does as a business." To ensure an adequate random sample of participants, BMSF funded Iraq and Afghanistan Veterans of America (IAVA) to recruit participants in the study. Thanks to IAVA's advertisement and endorsement, 275 veterans signed up to participate within 24 hours of the site going live. In this partnership, BMSF is funding innovation and an efficacy evaluation that healthcare providers will rely on to make future funding decisions.

Such work is not cheap. Rush University will receive nearly $600,000 to conduct the study, and IAVA received nearly $200,000 to recruit patients and ultimately produce a report on the findings. If the research provides definitive proof of program effectiveness, though, and helps inform the decision making of other funders, it will be money well spent.

Demanding Rigor in a New Program

Just before Grimes began her work at the foundation, she heard Barbara Van Dahlen, the founder of Give an Hour, speak at a conference of the American Psychiatric Foundation. While Van Dahlen's work with Give an Hour centered on matching volunteer mental-health professionals with veterans in need (see case 12), she was also working on a new idea for coordinating local services for veterans.

It was called the Community Blueprint, and the concept was to have localities provide packages of support services to veterans, servicemembers, and their families. "It sounded like a good model," says Damonti, "but no one had operationalized it to see what works, what doesn't work, what are the things you should think about. How do you bring community groups together around veteran issues?"

It was a good match for BMSF. Van Dahlen had an innovative idea. It needed to be tested, and then its lessons shared nationally.

BMSF didn't just cut a check and hope for the best. Grimes worked with Van Dahlen to refine the grant. "Barbara is a huge visionary—she wanted to go national, she wanted to roll it out. But we said, 'We're all about targeted programs—testing things before you expand them. So what do you think about developing it, then partnering with one or two communities to really evaluate it?' She totally got it. Most of our grantees really appreciate our ability to help them focus." Damonti continues, "So the initial grant we made to Give an Hour was to go to two very large military communities—Norfolk, Virginia, and Fayetteville, North Carolina—to model the Blueprint, put it to work, and kick the tires on the thing."

With a keen eye on outcomes, BMSF helped Give an Hour design a before-and-after survey of military families to measure the Community Blueprint's effects. Grimes and the BMSF team also required Give an Hour to develop a step-by-step manual encapsulating what was learned in these pilots. Taken together, these will help any future funders or organizations aiming to replicate the Blueprint.

Since BMSF's initial investment of approximately $1.9 million in late 2011, the Community Blueprint has attracted a five-year, $5 million commitment from the defense technology firm ITT Exelis. Several more communities have lined up to institute the Blueprint. And there are ambitious goals to bring the Blueprint's mode of organizing services for veterans to 400 communities within the next few years.

The Scientific Approach

Other grants in BMSF's mental-health portfolio run the gamut: behavioral interventions for disabled veterans, family education for veterans at risk of suicide, peer advisors for veterans on college campuses, intimate-partner violence prevention, and care for homeless female veterans, among other topics. Asked why BMSF funds such a wide variety of projects focusing on different subpopulations, Damonti answers in true BMSF fashion:

> When you work for a healthcare company, you don't do a clinical trial for heart disease on 5,000 men, look at the results and say, "Okay, this is going to work on a woman." Strategies have to be developed for specific populations because the complications of, for instance, getting young males and females to treatment are different.

By adhering strictly to its roots as the philanthropic arm of a rigorously science-based company, the Bristol-Myers Squibb Foundation has thus carved out a distinctive niche for itself. It is a niche that will yield benefits not only to veterans, servicemembers, and their families—but also to fellow donors who want to be sure that, when they reach out a friendly hand to those populations, they are actually helping.

FAMILY LIFE

Adding Veterans to a Prior Agenda
Blue Shield of California battles domestic violence

"We're not a foundation that had previously invested directly in military families," states Bess Bendet of the Blue Shield of California Foundation (BSCF). Each year, the foundation receives $25–$40 million from its corporate parent (Blue Shield of California) and most of this is donated to two causes: increasing healthcare access, and reducing domestic violence. As California's largest private funder of domestic violence services, BSCF keeps shelters open, educates high-risk populations on how to keep relationships healthy, and funds research. The foundation has contributed more than $40 million to the cause of domestic violence since 2002.

Back in 2008, when thinking about new populations the foundation could serve, Bendet began to "wonder about military families, if we could help in terms of preventing violence, because combat seems to create a lot of challenges that affect families." About a year later, several of the foundation's grantees began reporting anecdotally that they noticed increases in the number of military families experiencing relationship stress and conflict, and that these families' experiences seemed different from civilian ones.

In 2009, BSCF started giving grants for research on helping military families avoid domestic violence, donating more than $2 million to the subject in their first three years. Very little was known concretely about this problem. And although Bendet had some contacts with family advocacy programs on local bases, they were nervous because "they thought we were going to produce a bad press story about violence in military families."

Initially, the foundation struggled to bring the military community together with domestic-violence service providers. Getting over cultural and even vocabulary barriers proved difficult. It became clear this topic had not been addressed systematically. Rather than deterring, though, this motivated the

> The Blue Shield of California Foundation first measured the problem, then linked families to organizations that can help.

foundation to invest in new research and programs that could bridge the gap. It asked: "What tools do families need to ensure that their relationships are healthy during reintegration after tours of duty?"

What Is the Scope of the Problem?

When it came to basic questions about the level of family violence in military families, says Bendet, "We found no one was counting. The data that was available was from prior wars, so the most often-cited statistics on family violence were from Vietnam. There was no way the V.A. or Defense Department was going to make any decisions about services without data from today's wars," she explains. So "we decided to document domestic violence in the context of post-combat trauma."

First, the foundation funded Blue Star Families, a chapter-based organization for military parents (see case 18), to include in its annual household survey questions about incidents of domestic violence. Alongside that survey,

BSCF funded an independent research center co-located with the San Francisco V.A. hospital to conduct the first-ever large-scale study of the prevalence of domestic violence in post-9/11 military families. Finally, BSCF funded the San Jose State University Research Foundation to determine the prevalence of intimate partner violence on college campuses in California.

Collectively, these three investigations painted the first authoritative and up-to-date portrait of this subject. The studies found that higher rates of family violence correlate with post-traumatic stress, rather than with military culture or with deployment experiences as a whole. By nailing down those important distinctions through its research investments, the foundation has developed a body of evidence that other private philanthropists and public agencies can now use to make intelligent funding choices addressing family violence.

Introducing Prevention into Existing Relationships

Beyond research, BSCF has funded pilot programs that insert violence prevention into various programs and agencies that already work with military families. For instance, one BSCF grant to the organization Swords to Plowshares provided training to police departments across the state of California. Bendet explains that "police are first responders—if you get a call to a family situation at a house and it involves someone who's been in the military, the way you approach it might be different." At San Jose State University, BSCF funded the development of two anti-violence programs, Warriors at Home, and Loving a Veteran, which have been rolled out on community-college and university campuses throughout the state.

In another grant, BSCF funded the National Center on Family Homelessness to develop and evaluate a couples-based violence-prevention program specifically for military families. "It is a 12-session intensive program for couples developed by experts in military family wellness. Initial results are very promising," says Bendet.

This pioneering work of the Blue Shield of California Foundation shows how private philanthropy can bring to light previously unaddressed issues. Rather than forcing its funding priorities onto the field, the foundation started with a question: Just how much does domestic violence affect military families that have experienced combat deployments? Since no current evidence existed, the foundation built accurate answers with a range of partners—independent and university researchers, a military family organization, and a domestic-violence service organization. Using organizations that were already working with military families, BSCF then developed and evaluated prevention programs. Now, rather than flying blind, agencies devoted to helping the families of servicemembers and veterans have tools to work with.

Making School Work for Military Kids

Lockheed Martin and other donors ace an AP test

In 2010, we were in Hawaii meeting with schools, and one general who was about to be deployed to Afghanistan said to us, "There is no greater thing that you could do for me than to get this program in the schools here so you can take care of my family. While I'm deployed, I need my kids to get the highest quality education. That's what you can do for me." It's pretty compelling when it's coming from someone who is about to be sent to war for nine months away from his family.

—Gregg Fleisher,
National Math and Science Initiative

The general quoted above was talking about the Initiative for Military Families, a program that helps schools serving military families improve their students' performance on science- and math-related AP exams. In 2010, its first year, the initiative increased the number of students enrolled in AP math and science classes by 57 percent in its four pilot schools; by 2012 the program had been expanded to 52 schools, with similar strong uptake from students. In schools that implement the program, the number of passing AP scores typically comes close to doubling in the first year. And gains among students traditionally underrepresented in science and math success—girls, Hispanics, African Americans—roughly track the overall results.

The Initiative for Military Families was launched with $900,000 of initial funding from the Lockheed Martin Corporation, and is run by the National Math and Science Initiative. NMSI is a nonprofit organization founded in 2007 by leaders in business, education, and science to improve U.S. math and science schooling. NMSI has trained teachers, enriched curricula, recruited top college students to teach math and science, and raised Advanced Placement participation and scores in 462 schools locate in 18 states. The group has received institutional funding from Exxon Mobil Corporation, BAE Systems, the Bill & Melinda Gates Foundation, the Michael & Susan Dell Foundation, the Carnegie Corporation of New York, and many other donors.

The Initiative for Military Families didn't rack up its initial successes as a completely novel program; it hit the ground running as a spin-off of NMSI's existing effort aimed at non-military kids—its AP Training and Incentive Program, which is set up to increase the number of students who take and pass Advanced Placement tests in math, science, and English. Getting students to pass those exams is one of the best ways of increasing the flow of students into science, technology, engineering, or math majors in college—areas that are undersupplied in the U.S. economy.

NMSI helps schools prepare their students for the AP exams well before they step into their first high school class. It brings in curriculum specialists to help schools reach back as far as sixth grade and lines up a sequence of courses that can culminate in AP success. It conducts site visits to identify which teachers best fit the program, train teachers over the summer, mentor them throughout the school year, and provide cash incentives to teachers of $100 for every student who passes an AP exam.

In addition to having the benefit of well-prepped teachers, students in the program attend extra study sessions outside of class hours. And they are provided their own cash rewards of $100 if they succeed on the test. All NMSI schools must allow every interested student the opportunity to take an AP

> **"**There is no greater thing you can do for me while I'm deployed than to take care of my family," said a general.

class. "Teachers have to think differently about who is an AP kid," says Lynn Gibson of NMSI.

One of the mottos of the National Math and Science Initiative is: "We don't reinvent wheels, we find the best ones—and roll." Its AP program is based on a system developed in the Dallas Independent School District in the late 1990s. Before implementation, only 26 African-American students in that district earned a passing score on their AP exams; by 2012, over 1,100 did. NMSI's AP offshoot is currently being implemented in 462 schools around the country, 52 of which fall under the Initiative for Military Families.

A Natural Fit

In 2009, the chairman of the National Math and Science Initiative, Tom Luce, contacted Pete Geren, an old friend who was then Secretary of the Army, with an idea—he thought NMSI's AP program would be beneficial for military families. Geren had already been addressing the educational needs of military families. He explains that "because of the itinerant nature of life in the Army, education is forever a problem for military families. Not only do they move all the time, but they move between schools with different education systems and different levels of quality."

Geren had been working with state legislatures around the country on an interstate compact that made it easier for military students to transfer between schools in different states without being penalized for missing state-specific requirements; by the end of 2012, all but a few states had signed on. That, however, couldn't eliminate variations in curriculum, and styles and quality of instruction, that sometimes trip up students from military families after they arrive from other locales. So Geren thought the extra boost toward AP success that the NMSI program would supply might be very helpful to the children of soldiers.

"When somebody moves from one base to the next and sees teachers with the same type of training, and classes with the same type of curriculum, it's something that they can rely on for consistent offerings. It's so sorely needed," explains Gregg Fleisher of NMSI.

By bringing consistent, high-quality math, science, and English curricula for grades 6–12 to many of the school districts where military families congregate, the NMSI program eliminates big structural obstacles that children of servicemembers would otherwise face when the military reassigns their parents to a different state or country. Even students who don't themselves follow an AP track benefit from schools voluntarily establishing subject curricula that are consistent from place to place. Students find educational continuity within a sometimes tumultuous lifestyle.

"It's helpful for military children to participate in these programs in some ways more than other children we work with, because they have to move, and NMSI makes school continuity and quality one less thing for them to worry about," says Gibson.

NMSI aims to eventually bring the program to 150 schools with heavy military populations. That's roughly the entire collection of public schools serving big numbers of military children around the country. When Geren first heard about Luce's expansion plan, he thought, "I admire your ambition but I just can't imagine that could ever get done—every school district and every school would be a separate project."

The expansion so far, though, has been rapid. In its first year, the Initiative for Military Families was piloted in four schools. In 2011, that increased to 29 schools in 10 states. In 2012, the program was in 52 schools spanning 15 states. In just three years, the organization was more than one-third of the way to its goal. To carry out this aggressive plan, NMSI enlisted the help of several partners and adjusted its program slightly to accommodate the unique circumstances of the military community.

Major funders like Lockheed Martin, Boeing, BAE Systems, and Northrop Grumman backed the program from the beginning. When the Department of Defense saw the initiative's results, it also became a funder in the program's second year. Schools must have at least 15 percent military dependents to quality for the DoD funding.

Though spending varies slightly by location, bringing the program to a typical school costs NMSI $450,000 over three years to train and compensate teachers and students. After that point it becomes self-sustaining. The cost comes to about $200 per year for each student touched by the program.

When Lockheed Martin provided the major gift that allowed the National Math and Science Initiative to bring this breakthrough to the children of servicemembers, it and its funding partners broke new ground. A regimen that had originally been designed for low-performing schools was transferred to schools where the issue was students who move every few years. And the model turned out to be even more effective in these schools with lots of military kids.

Philanthropists aspiring to help military families and veterans should work to minimize structural penalties and barriers created by military service. By virtue of their parents' active-duty military service, military children have access to much less consistent education than their civilian peers. By taking action, Lockheed Martin and NMSI made life much less uncertain for these students. If they move any time after the sixth grade between public schools participating in the Initiative for Military Families, even across the country, military children can now expect to find approximately the same high-quality curriculum and instruction on roughly the same schedule. That is a gift for children and parents both, and it's producing graduates much better prepared for work in a technical world.

FAMILY LIFE

Meeting Military Families Where They Live

A universe of givers births
Blue Star Families

In late 2008, seven military spouses from different places, service branches, deployment cycles, and phases of
life met by happenstance and realized that, while the
military is a supportive community, there was work
to be done in meeting some of the needs of military
families. The new organization they formed that year
is called Blue Star Families. "Military families are not
always set up to cross-pollinate, because of geographic
dispersion," says co-founder Vivian Greentree. While
official Family Readiness Groups effectively support

families during their servicemembers' deployments, little exists to help connect families between deployments, or across service branches, or in different career stages, never mind through the servicemember's process of reintegrating into civilian life.

Beyond the humanitarian value of increasing life quality for military families, there is a national interest in protecting the well-being of these households, Greentree notes. "If we want to continue to have an all-volunteer force, we need people who want to volunteer. A lot of them have families. These bright leaders that the military has trained will not stay in if their spouses can't progress in their own career, or if their kids don't have the resources they need."

As a local chapter-based organization, Blue Star Families focuses on "supporting, connecting, and empowering" military families. Once linked with lots of their peers, families can help themselves. The organization also provides some direct programming to military families. In the first four years of its life, the group grew to 31 chapters based mostly at military installations, and serving thousands of military family members around the globe.

For Us, by Us

The staff of Blue Star Families spans nine time zones. As executive director Mark Smith says, "That's where military families are." Every member of its 16-person staff is a veteran, family member of a veteran, or a military spouse, who directly understand the needs of military families because they live the life themselves every day.

That's how the organization's Books on Bases program sprang up. "Base libraries are notoriously underfunded and don't have the best selections," explains Greentree. "So what can we do about that? We decided to get a donor to come and donate books." With corporate philanthropic support from McDonald's, Disney, and several publishers, Blue Star Families has donated 100,000 books to military children through local base chapters in just two years.

Blue Star Museums is another popular program that bloomed quickly with philanthropic support. Blue Star CEO Kathy Roth-Douquet had already been taking her kids to museums as a way to get through their father's deployments. Of course, museum tickets can be expensive, so some military families could not afford to do this often. In 2009, the MetLife Foundation underwrote the costs of administering a new program in which museums around the country agree to offer free admission or special programming for military family members between Memorial Day and Labor Day.

Blue Star Families advertised the program among military families, and it was a hit. In the latest year, the program's third, more than 450,000 participants visited about 1,800 museums during the four-month open season. "I can take my kids to a museum and say, 'They're doing this for us because your dad is serving,'" explains Greentree.

The secret to the popularity of Blue Star's programming is its focus on eliciting and responding to the needs of its constituents. It conducts an annual survey of military families, collecting and publishing responses on a wide range of challenges, opportunities, attitudes, and concerns. In its 2013 survey, the group sampled 5,125 respondents from a wide range of backgrounds.

The survey has been funded by donors like the Blue Shield of California Foundation. Part of what attracted the foundation to Blue Star Families was its "for us, by us" nature. The group's members represent themselves, without filtering by third parties.

Because BSF is an independent organization, its Military Family Lifestyle Survey has the freedom to ask many questions that Department of Defense

> The staff of Blue Star Families all live the life themselves, so they understand the needs of military families.

surveys do not. In addition to yielding important demographic and attitudinal data on military family life, the annual survey is the primary tool by which BSF charts its work.

BSF's first survey revealed that 95 percent of respondents felt that most civilians did not understand their service. One day, the kindness of one of Greentree's neighbors gave her an idea for how the group might respond. "One of my sons got a letter from a neighbor while my husband was deployed and it said, 'You're doing a great job. Keep it up.' It was so touching." There are many programs that send letters to servicemembers. But there were none that allowed people to write letters to military families showing their support. Operation Appreciation was born, and subsequently grew rapidly. Greentree sees it as more than just a chance for emotional venting; it is an opportunity to bridge the civil-military divide in a very concrete way.

Addressing the Whole Family, not Just the Servicemember

The annual survey, which continues to be funded by donors, has inspired other initiatives. The 2012 questionnaire found that among the families polled, 26 percent of the military spouses who wanted to work were unemployed. While many programs, philanthropic and governmental alike, have been created in recent years to address unemployment among veterans, this problem that military spouses have in finding work is rarely understood, much less ameliorated.

Frequent moves, spousal absences, and other factors are behind this difficulty in finding good work. The Blue Star survey showed that many spouses balance these difficulties by volunteering at higher than normal rates. Unfortunately, according to the BSF survey, only two-thirds of the spouses found their volunteer experience useful when looking for a job. Greentree saw a gap to fill.

"We began working with Hiring Our Heroes and the Military Spouse Employment Partnership, because they have access to private companies who want to hire military spouses. No amount of job fairs, though, would bridge the gap if spouses aren't bringing in competitive résumés. And they aren't competitive if they leave off the majority of their volunteer experience. Our surveys consistently show that military spouses are volunteering at incredible rates, building skills in the process that employers can use. So we got together a group of volunteers and said 'We're going to put together a résumé translator.'" With funding from Hiring Our Heroes, Blue Star created a mechanism for translating common volunteer experiences within military families into terms understandable by commercial employers.

BSF also found that many military families have little help during transitions—adjusting to a deployment, the servicemember's return, a move to a new base, the transition to civilian life. With support from CBS and Vulcan Productions, Blue Star created a Family Reintegration Toolkit. It offers information on what to expect, and advice on how to navigate different phases. The handbook includes very concrete checklists, information on resources available, and vignettes of family life throughout the military lifecycle. The first edition was distributed in hard cover to 300,000 military families across the country.

Noeleen Tillman, managing director of BSF, anticipates continuing demand for the toolkit. "Many military families expected to have a long career, but given the drawdown now on the horizon, there won't be opportunities for a lot of them." Additional donations from several sources, including NBC Universal and the Wounded Warrior Project, have allowed the group to update and expand the toolkit and convert it into an e-book for wider distribution starting in 2013. Asked why Blue Star Families chose to focus on this, Tillman responds that this subject "came back as a high priority in our survey. We build our programs around what our members need."

19

LEGAL

Fixing Legal Troubles at Low Cost

Connecticut supporters give vets a center for help with the law

"I'm facing eviction because my truck broke down and it was literally either fix my truck, which is the thing that gets me to work, or I could pay my rent. So I fixed my truck, and I've been going to work, but I missed half my rent last month and my landlord has served me a notice of eviction and I can't go back to being homeless because I can't do that to my daughter again."

That was the predicament of an Iraq-war veteran and single mother with a four-year-old daughter who became a client of the Connecticut Veterans Legal Center (CVLC). "A V.A. clinician put her in touch with us," says Margaret Middleton, CVLC's executive director, "so we connected this veteran with a volunteer attorney who had not done a landlord-tenant case before but who said, 'I'm a litigator, we'll be alright.'" The attorney negotiated a repayment plan with the landlord in which the veteran repaid a small portion of her back rent each month until the debt was cleared. In the end, Middleton concludes, "It wasn't a ton of work for the volunteer attorney, it wasn't a ton of work for us, and as a team, we prevented this veteran and her daughter from becoming homeless."

While not every case is quite so picture-perfect, this one showcases much of what makes CVLC tick—recruiting volunteer attorneys from across the state, forming a strong referral relationship with the V.A., and quickly addressing a broad range of practical legal issues that can complicate the reintegration of veterans into civilian society. Founded in late 2009, the nonprofit organization is built on *pro bono* services donated by lawyers, with administrative funding from local family and community foundations. It has so far opened more than 822 cases on behalf of about 600 clients. According to Middleton, there is much more work to be done.

Legal Problems among Veterans

In the realm of services for veterans, recognizing and removing legal obstacles has rarely been a top priority. Even lawyers willing to help have often been frustrated in their efforts to make useful volunteer connections to needy clients. By the time CVLC was founded, the Connecticut Bar Association had been trying to start a veterans project for several years, but could never find the veterans they aimed to serve. Sustained by philanthropic support from over a dozen Connecticut law firms, as well as family and community foundations, CVLC tried something different—going to the places where veterans congregate. Now that the project is up and running, Middleton reports, "we're awash in veterans. We have way more demand than we can serve."

While CVLC is not a government office, it is co-located and well-synchronized with the V.A.'s Errera Community Care Center in West Haven, where veterans access counseling resources, receive substance abuse treatment, obtain housing help, and other services. CVLC's mission is to "help veterans overcome legal barriers to housing, health care, and income," often serving as the connective tissue between other parts of the recovery of veterans who have run into trouble. Middleton explains:

Legal problems are barriers to recovery, so folks who are trying to establish sobriety, be faithful to their treatment plans, trying to maintain housing, sometimes run into legal problems they can't resolve on their own. There are other legal services in V.A. facilities, but we are built into the fabric, and we're proving that clinicians, veterans, and lawyers can work together without violating patient or client confidentiality. It's beneficial to the veterans and the clinicians love having us here—when their client asks them a question, they have someone they can direct them to.

The West Haven V.A. recognizes the value of CVLC's work and provides it with some in-kind support. "The government provides us with space, wi-fi, phones, copy machines, and security. If we were a storefront, our clients would have a harder time reaching us and we wouldn't get the benefits of working with their clinicians." By working on-site in partnership with V.A. services, CVLC has been able to help more veterans in more ways than most other legal services programs.

Middleton says the organization particularly zeroed in on hard cases—"veterans who are recovering from homelessness and serious mental illness." Their single largest legal need is for help navigating V.A. benefits, but other issues such as family law, housing law, discharge upgrades, administrative pardons, and identity theft make up significant portions of the CVLC caseload.

Among Iraq-Afghanistan veterans—who constitute about 20 percent of the total clients of this charity—the single largest area of need is in family law. "A lot of these are young people with young kids, and military service is incredibly straining on family life. There are a lot of issues with child support and custody."

Lawyering for the Greater Good

Working out of a single 150 square-foot office at the West Haven V.A. with two staff attorneys, one paralegal, and an AmeriCorps fellow, CVLC has served more than 600 clients in less than four years. In 2012 alone, the group opened 400 new cases. Unable to handle the flow of work on their own, the group farms its cases out to a network of about 238 volunteer attorneys, paralegals, and law students around the state of Connecticut who take on the cases *pro bono*.

CVLC doesn't just hand cases off; they match needs with attorneys, and remain actively involved in cases right through case resolution. All told, it costs the organization an average of $450 to complete an entire case—the rate some private attorneys charge for just one hour of time. And the client never pays a dime for CVLC's services. In the latest year alone, the estimated value of billable time donated by the organization's volunteer attorneys surpassed $400,000, more than twice CVLC's cash budget for that same time period.

CVLC delivers this value by recruiting volunteer lawyers from a wide variety of firms, law schools, corporations, and practices around the state. In conjunction with Yale Law School just up the road from CVLC, Middleton runs regular training sessions for these attorneys, who are often new to working with veterans, and to the particular practice areas, where their legal needs tend to be concentrated. While some issue areas, such as family law and certain V.A. benefits appeals, require specialized experience, most do not.

In many cases, Middleton explains, CVLC "is tapping into their innate talent as lawyers to overcome fairly routine stuff. We work with a lot of corporate lawyers—at Sikorsky, at GE—doing pardons. These are great projects for in-house counsel because they are largely paper processes that don't require repeated court appearances, and they're not intensely technical. They're mostly about helping a veteran tell a story of growth, healing, and redemption."

In addition to putting volunteerism among practicing attorneys to good use, CVLC also taps into a pool of talented students training to be lawyers. About a year after Middleton founded CVLC, Mike Wishnie, a professor at Yale Law School, started a legal clinic at his school as a way to teach his students, provide them with real experience in litigation and advocacy, and help a population in need in the local community. He quickly made common cause with Middleton, who now helps supervise the students in the clinic and offers referrals. She is a "source of expertise, and students consult with her constantly," says Wishnie.

Teaching Courts to Serve Veterans

Outside of directly serving clients on individual cases, CVLC has also had a constructive influence in the Connecticut courts system on behalf of veterans. Since they were first piloted in Buffalo, New York, in 2008, specialized courts for veterans that provide treatment alternatives to incarceration for individuals facing criminal charges have proliferated around the country. So-called Veterans Treatment Courts (VTCs) bring together drug-treatment programs, mental-health providers,

> Over the last year, the estimated value of billable time donated by CVLC's volunteer attorneys was more than twice its cash budget.

community agencies, corrections offices, and the V.A. to rehabilitate veterans. By many accounts, they have worked well where established in law.

But these new freestanding courts cost local governments money to set up, so they do not exist in every jurisdiction. For years, advocates for veterans and Linda Schwartz, the commissioner of the Connecticut Department of Veterans Affairs, tried to establish a VTC in their state. But they were never able to overcome political, budgetary, and bureaucratic obstacles.

So in 2011, Middleton asked some of the students she was working with at the Yale Law School clinic for veterans to research practical options for bringing a VTC to Connecticut. After several months of work the students came back and suggested: "Let's go to the legislature and just work with existing programs; not create something new, but tweak them." Wishnie explains that "pre-trial diversionary programs" already operate in Connecticut, and "are successful, and save the state money because it's cheaper to treat someone than incarcerate them. But they all have various limitations." In early 2012, CVLC retained the law school clinic as legislative counsel, and the students, under Wishnie's supervision, wrote what would become S.B. 114, a bill that modified an existing statute to make pre-trial treatment opportunities available to veterans, where in the past only defendants with psychiatric disabilities had been eligible.

By expanding the access of veterans to treatment courts, CVLC also helped reduce future barriers to employment. "A lot of vets coming back want to be police officers, want to work in security, they want to maintain a security clearance." For this to remain possible, it was helpful for veterans with substance-abuse problems to be able to get connected to care without resorting to the old law's requirement that one demonstrate a psychiatric disability.

The bill was passed into law in May 2012. Unlike VTCs, which are by definition new courts, S.B. 114 expanded access for veterans throughout the state of Connecticut to existing pre-trial diversionary programs. Middleton elaborates, "It's a very different model than what you're seeing in most places that are creating veterans courts. Philosophically we prefer Connecticut's law, because it creates the potential for every court to be a veterans court. Every judge, every prosecutor, every defense attorney has the opportunity to say 'this person is a veteran and because of their service we're going to make sure they get every opportunity to receive treatment.'" Because the programs have been around for years, judges around the state already have some familiarity with them and are simply applying them to a new population.

Doing a Lot with a Little

When CVLC solves a legal problem for a veteran, it also often plays a supporting role in encouraging other successful outcomes like getting a job and finding housing. One of CVLC's biggest donors is the Community Foundation for Greater New Haven. Its director, William Ginsberg, describes the organization as "a very important program. They're doing very good work; and they're doing it in ways that leverage our dollars hugely with volunteers, and with the work of the V.A. hospital in West Haven."

Wishnie concurs: "It would be great if there were more CVLCs—either as small, free-standing legal services offices, or as programs of existing legal clinics. When philanthropically financed lawyers are doing cases, or intelligently matching cases to *pro bono* lawyers, and working with local law-school clinics, then you're leveraging a lot of resources for a fairly small budget."

FINANCIAL

A Business-like Approach to Philanthropy
Wachovia, Citi, and Ryder help VeteransPlus teach family finance

Financial literacy is not the most emotionally evocative subject for philanthropists interested in veterans. Challenges like amputations and unemployment conjure compelling images; financial literacy, by comparison, sounds boring. It is, however, a highly relevant issue for hundreds of thousands of current or former servicemembers and their families. Whether it shows up in household spending, identify theft, security-clearance complications, loan problems, or simply getting over the hump of emergency expenses, financial capacities can make the difference between retaining and losing a job, house, or family. That's why a group called VeteransPlus, with support from some banks and other donors, has recently begun to provide financial education and counseling specifically designed for veterans, servicemembers, and their families.

"I would see people make poor decisions simply because they didn't know how to budget, calculate their credit scores, protect their financial privacy. In spite of all the benefits that other nonprofits and the federal government provide, financial literacy seemed to be something that was missing," recalls John Pickens, executive director of VeteransPlus.

The organization started locally in 2009, delivering basic home-finance workshops to veterans in locations around Florida. Soon, however, the team realized that individuals and families faced a variety of money-management challenges throughout their military careers: enlistment bonuses, combat pay, expenses related to deployment or station transfers, jumps from civilian work to National Guard or Reserve deployment, injury-related changes in earning potential, and delays in government payments could wreak havoc on household budgets.

VeteransPlus developed Ready, Aim, Fire, a program for teaching money management at various stages of deployment. Ready, the pre-deployment curriculum, helps servicemembers get their financial affairs in order prior to deployment; Aim provides support and guidance during deployments, mostly to military spouses facing increased financial responsibilities; and Fire offers help in making wise choices during the transition after deployment. Recognizing the value of the program early on, Wachovia (since acquired by Wells Fargo) funded VeteransPlus to send its counselors on a national tour with the goal of reaching 3,000 individuals in workshops in 22 states.

At the same time, the Defense Department office providing support to National Guard and Reserve members invited VeteransPlus to present at 1,500 financial workshops in a single year. The VeteransPlus counselors thus became involved in several workshops at each city stop. In 2012 alone, the organization served 9,400 clients in these seminars.

While these seminars experienced prolific growth, Pickens explains that "no one is going to raise a hand in a workshop and say, 'Hey I'm $20,000 in debt and can't pay my bills, can you talk with me?'" So the group started one-on-one counseling sessions, "so that after we provide the education, they can have somebody to talk to at length, do an assessment, and show them the elements of a budget." Discovering that clients often resisted face-to-face counseling for the same reasons they would not raise their hands in a workshop, VeteransPlus nimbly shifted to a call-center model. "They're comfortable calling from home when their kids are in bed and their bills are on the kitchen table," says Pickens, at which points they can put pen to paper with a counselor by phone and work through assets, income, expenses, and liabilities.

The organization prides itself on providing counselors who are veterans or military family members and have received professional certifications pertinent to their specialties. In 2012, these certified counselors conducted one-on-one counseling with nearly 5,000 vets and servicemembers.

Bringing Order to Emergency Aid

While it was offering clients these tools for sustaining long-term financial health, VeteransPlus also carved a niche in providing emergency aid. Many charities are willing to offer assistance to military families facing an immediate cash crunch, but few use any methodical verification or means test to ensure that the need is legitimate, has not already been met by some other organization, and is complemented with the right type of financial counseling to help individuals and families get back on their feet.

So, VeteransPlus struck up a partnership with several aid organizations in what is called the Yellow Ribbon Registry Network. It operates as both a website for matching applicants with assistance organizations, and an association of assistance organizations dedicated to avoiding misuse of charitable aid. Organizations providing emergency financial assistance through the network refer applicants to VeteransPlus for an in-depth analysis of their applications and financial circumstances, as well as counseling and financial education. The information VeteransPlus collects can then be used by the charities to inform their decisions on assistance.

After several of these organizations had joined Yellow Ribbon Registry Network, the VeteransPlus team noticed "people come in from one partner, and then three months later they would go to another partner." Whether they were actively gaming the system or just relying on aid without fixing their longer-term problems, this was not healthy behavior. The Registry Network eliminates both risks by imposing some order on the private financial-assistance landscape.

Good information on each applicant is gathered and then shared among all of the charities via a dashboard. "They can see who they're helping, who our other partners on the network are helping, and they can collaborate with each other." This helps make sure that the right amount of assistance gets to the right recipients in the right way.

At the same time, the Registry Network makes sure all recipients of emergency aid get counseling on how to keep themselves out of financial crunches in the future. They also get help navigating the short-term aid system. Many assistance organizations have different eligibility requirements, making it tricky to apply. Applicants often had to submit multiple applications to raise their chances of hearing back from one.

The Yellow Ribbon Registry uses a common application for emergency aid, and directs households only to the programs they qualify for. Applicants "can see where their request is in process—who has accepted it, who is considering it," says Pickens. Since its launch in 2011, the network has helped its partners process more than 6,800 applications for emergency financial assistance, 70 percent of which were granted.

VeteransPlus is able to follow up with these recipients, offer counseling, and make sure they haven't fallen back into old habits. As part of its agreement with the PenFed Foundation, for instance, VeteransPlus takes each client through a counseling session before the money is disbursed, and then checks

> VeteransPlus follows up with aid recipients, offers counseling, and makes sure they haven't fallen back into old habits.

in 45 days later to see what types of financial adjustments and decisions recipients have made. In its work screening applicants to Habitat for Humanity, VeteransPlus offers "rehabilitative" financial counseling to all veterans who do not qualify for a Habitat house. If their VeteransPlus counseling results in a steady record of improved performance, those families can later qualify for the Habitat for Humanity program.

Attracting Business-like Donors

The growth of VeteransPlus has been supported by major donors like Citigroup. Jamie Alderslade of Citi's community development arm explains that "the delivery of financial coaching and education for veterans is a priority for us." The bank's Citi Salutes program is its veterans initiative, combining strands that aim to hire veterans, to provide mortgage and banking services to veterans and servicemembers, and to offer philanthropic help in various forms. Alderslade says the company looks for ways to "support individuals to make positive financial decisions throughout their lives, rather than just at a moment in time." After finding very few veterans organizations that met that standard,

Citi has embraced VeteransPlus, supporting the nonprofit at up to $50,000 annually for several years now.

Another example of a company drawn to VeteransPlus in its corporate giving is Ryder, the large truck-rental and logistics company. As a business oriented toward helping customers make smart decisions about, say, purchasing versus leasing a fleet of vehicles, Ryder is interested in financial efficiency. When it came to their corporate philanthropy they identified VeteransPlus as a kindred spirit.

Ryder particularly values the way the Yellow Ribbon Registry Network has reduced inefficiencies and abuse in the provision of emergency aid to military families. In addition to providing financial support for the project, Ryder donated one of its own IT teams to help VeteransPlus set up the registry's computer system—to ensure it had adequate data protection measures in place to safeguard its clients' information, just as Ryder does with the businesses and individuals renting its equipment. "When we heard how difficult it was for philanthropic funding to reach the right veterans in time, it made perfect sense," says David Bruce of Ryder.

VITAL
STATISTICS

Population of Servicemembers and Veterans

A little fewer than 2.5 million servicemembers served in Iraq or Afghanistan, 28 percent from Reserves or National Guard. Over a million individuals were deployed more than once. Among all veterans in the U.S. right now, the group who served after the 9/11 attacks is less than 13 percent.

Current armed forces	2,767,000
Active duty	1,457,000
Troops currently deployed overseas for war on terror	168,000
Troops currently in Afghanistan	65,000
Total deployments for Iraq/Afghanistan wars	**4,231,000**
Servicemembers who were deployed to Iraq or Afghanistan at least once	2,444,000
Active duty	1,753,000
National Guard and Reserve	691,000
Servicemembers deployed more than once	1,040,000
U.S. veterans currently in civilian life, by era they served[1]	**22,328,000**
Iraq/Afghanistan war era	3,210,220
Male	2,560,000
Female	651,000
Gulf War era	4,243,000
Vietnam War era	7,489,000
Korean War era	2,273,000
World War II era	1,396,000
Served in peacetime	5,622,000

1. Sum of sub-totals is greater than total living veterans because those who served in multiple conflicts are counted during each period of service.

Sources: DoD Office of Deputy Under Secretary of Defense for Military Community and Family Policy, "2011 Demographics: Profile of the Military Community"; Defense Manpower Data Center, "Contingency Tracking System Deployment File"; V.A., "Veteran Population Projection Model 2011."

Employment Status

Of the roughly 2.5 million men and women who served during the war on terror and are now out of the military, 19 percent are not in the labor force—they are at college, raising children, retired. Of the remainder who are in the labor force, 90 percent are employed, and 10 percent are unemployed (their jobless rate being about two percentage points higher than non-veterans). Older vets are having better luck with jobs than younger ones (in fact, they have better employment rates than non-veterans), and men are doing better than women. Spouses of members of the military, who must deal with moves and deployments, face special challenges getting jobs. (All numbers below are 2012 annual averages, and cover all veterans who served in the post-9/11 period.)

Still serving in the military	2,767,000		
Active duty	1,457,000		
Post-9/11 veterans now in the civilian labor force[1]	2,071,000		
Employed	1,866,000		
Unemployed	205,000	9.9%	Compared to 7.9% for all non-veteran workers
Males unemployed	168,000	9.5%	Compared to 8.1% for non-veteran male workers
Females unemployed	37,000	12.5%	Compared to 7.7% for non-veteran female workers
Ages 18–24 unemployed	39,000	20.0%	Compared to 15.0% for non-veterans of the same age
Ages 25–34 unemployed	90,000	10.4%	Compared to 8.2% for non-veterans of the same age
Ages 35–54 unemployed	17,000	5.0%	Compared to 6.6% for non-veterans of the same age
Not in the labor force at present	496,000		
Spouses of current active-duty military who are unemployed	109,000	12–15%	

1. Includes National Guard and Reserve members with ongoing service commitments.

Sources: DoD Office of Deputy Under Secretary of Defense for Military Community and Family Policy, "2011 Demographics: Profile of the Military Community"; Bureau of Labor Statistics and Bureau of the Census, "Labor Force Statistics from the Current Population Survey."

Education and Human Capital

There is a common misperception that many of the Americans who volunteer for military service do so because they lack skills to make it in the civilian economy. Actually, the young people who serve today exceed national norms, on average, in education and intelligence, health, and character qualities. On the whole, it is most accurate to think of people who have served in the military as a national asset, rather than a problematic population.

Educational attainment of military servicemembers	Individuals	Rate	Comparable civilian rate
No high school diploma	27,000	1%	12%
High school, some college, or associate's degree	1,773,000	78%	59%
Bachelor's degree or higher	428,000	19%	29%
Military officers holding a B.A. or higher	304,000	83%	
Proportion of the population that meets prevailing intelligence, physical-fitness, criminal, and family standards for acceptance into the U.S. military	Americans serving in the military: 100% All young Americans: 25%		

Sources: DoD Office of Deputy Under Secretary of Defense for Military Community and Family Policy, "2011 Demographics: Profile of the Military Community"; U.S. Bureau of the Census, "Educational Attainment in the United States: 2012."

Physical Injuries

Nearly all Americans agree that our society should pull out all the stops to heal and rehabilitate men and women injured during military service, and to comfort the families of the fallen. Thanks to improved combat medicine, many of the wounded who would have died in past wars now survive—some of them requiring extended support during recovery. Fortunately, compared to the millions who served in Iraq or Afghanistan, the number seriously hurt is smaller than sometimes imagined, as totaled below. It is these on whom intensive care must be concentrated. (Unless otherwise noted, these numbers cumulate all injuries and deaths from the end of 2001 through early 2013.)

Deployment deaths during Iraq/Afghanistan war era[1]	6,641
Wounded in action	50,519
Combat injuries serious enough to result in evacuation from theater (through December 3, 2012)	14,788
Cumulative suicides by servicemembers (while in the U.S. or deployed)	2,744
Wounded-to-fatality ratio	
Iraq/Afghanistan war	8:1
Vietnam War	3:1
World War II	2:1
Iraq-Afghanistan servicemembers undergoing major amputations	1,715
Those with severe burns (2003–2013)	1,147
Injuries with high risk of blindness (2000–2010)	4,852
Complete blindness	approx. 250
Individuals with spinal-cord injuries (Oct. 2001–Dec. 2009)	104
Annual cases of sexual assault or rape reported (2011)	3,158
Estimate of unreported cases (2011)	15,800

---

1. Excludes suicides.

Sources: Defense Manpower Data Center, "Defense Casualty Analysis System"; Congressional Research Service, "U.S. Military Casualty Statistics: OND, OIF, OEF"; Armed Forces Health Surveillance Center, "June 2012 Medical Surveillance Monthly Report"; Institute of Medicine: "Returning Home from Iraq and Afghanistan"; U.S. Army Institute of Surgical Research; National Alliance for Eye and Vision Research; Journal of Bone & Joint Surgery, "Spinal Column Injuries Among Americans in the Global War on Terrorism"; DoD Sexual Assault Prevention and Response Office, "Annual Report on Sexual Assault in the Military."

Mental Health / Substance Abuse

Roadside bomb blasts caused significant numbers of concussions among recently deployed servicemembers, and some serious brain injuries. Post-traumatic stress diagnoses are rising (for reasons discussed in the introduction to this book). Alcohol use is higher among servicemembers and drug use is lower, compared to equivalent-age civilian counterparts. (Brain injuries and traumatic stress diagnoses are cumulated totals for the period 2002–2012.)

Servicemembers experiencing concussion or brain injury (while in the U.S. or deployed)		
Severe or penetrating brain injury		5,548
Concussion, mild to moderate brain injury		214,855
Servicemembers diagnosed with traumatic stress		155,037
9/11-era veterans diagnosed by V.A. with traumatic stress		239,174
Cases of depression in active-duty servicemembers (2011)		31,407
Heavy alcohol use within the past month[1] (2008)	Military rate	Civilian rate
Ages 18–25	26%	16%
Any illicit drug use within the past month (2008)	Military rate	Total U.S. rate
Ages 18–25	14%	20%
Prescription drug misuse within the past month		
Ages 18–25	10%	3%

1. Military and civilian definitions of heavy usage are not identical. If it was measured by the military definition (bingeing once a week over the last month), the civilian rate would be higher than 16 percent.

Sources: Congressional Research Service, "U.S. Military Casualty Statistics: OND, OIF, OEF"; V.A., "Report on V.A. Facility Specific OEF/OIF/OND Veterans Coded with Potential PTSD—Revised"; Armed Forces Health Surveillance Center, "June 2012 Medical Surveillance Monthly Report"; Institute of Medicine, "Substance Use Disorders in the U.S. Armed Forces."

Family and Community

About 2 million spouses and children share family life with full-time members of the military. Reservists and National Guard have another million or so family members. About 200,000 dependents have a family member deployed overseas right now. Single parents and dual-military parents, though not large in number, face special burdens.

Total dependents of military families	3,131,000
Active-duty dependents	1,985,000
Military spouses (active-duty, Reserve, and National Guard)	1,132,000
Children of servicemembers, by age:	
0–5	743,000
6–11	602,000
12–18	498,000
Dependents of servicemembers currently deployed in war on terror	190,000
Families of deceased servicemembers	9,700
Single parents in the military	155,000
Dual-military-parent households	52,000
Iraq/Afghanistan-era veterans living in urban communities (2010)	2,189,000
Iraq/Afghanistan-era veterans living in rural communities (2010)	1,020,000

Sources: DoD Office of Deputy Under Secretary of Defense for Military Community and Family Policy, "2011 Demographics: Profile of the Military Community"; Defense Manpower Data Center, "Defense Casualty Analysis System"; V.A., "Characteristics of Rural Veterans: 2010 American Community Survey."

Legal / Financial / Housing

Contrary to some popular misperceptions, military families are no more likely to divorce than other families, and their rate of single-parenting is far below the national average. Veterans are much less likely to be in poverty than the rest of the population, and more likely to earn high incomes. Populations of special concern, like the homeless, are of a size that should be manageable by effective programs.

	Individuals	Military rate	Civilian rate
Divorce occuring among active-duty military in 2011	29,458	4%	4%
Single parents in active-duty military in 2011	75,214	5%	17%
Veterans of all wars living in poverty in 2009	1,435,375	7%	13%
Veterans of all wars living at 400% of the poverty level in 2009	10,126,000	47%	39%
Median annual earnings of employed male veterans from all wars		$51,230	$45,811
Median annual earnings of employed female veterans from all wars		$41,441	$36,099
Homeless veterans (point-in-time count, January 2011)	67,000		

Sources: DoD Office of Deputy Under Secretary of Defense for Military Community and Family Policy, "2011 Demographics: Profile of the Military Community"; V.A., "Health Insurance Coverage, Poverty, and Income of Veterans: 2000 to 2009; V.A., "Profile of Veterans: 2009 Data from the American Community Survey"; V.A., "Homeless Veteran Point-in-Time Count by State."

WHAT
DONORS AND
CHARITIES
ARE DOING

While not exhaustive, this list outlines many of the major areas where veterans and servicemembers have needs that can be addressed through philanthropy.

The examples of donors and charities should not be treated as at all comprehensive, nor as an endorsement, but rather as a starting point for understanding the range of funders and service providers active in this field.

For ease of comparison, the list's pages are set up to mirror the list that follows: **What the Federal Government Provides**. Both lists are organized by the same topics at the top of each page, and the same need categories down the left side of the page. That will allow you to quickly compare the existing private and public footprints in every area as you plan your own philanthropy.

Employment

	Examples of service providers
Training and certification	Entrepreneurship Bootcamp for Veterans with Disabilities
	FastTrac for Veteran Entrepreneurs
	Workforce Opportunity Services
	Military Spouse Fellowships
	Project Return2Work
	Syracuse University Institute for Veterans and Military Families
	Swords to Plowshares
	The Manufacturing Institute
Placement	Hiring Our Heroes
	Hire America's Heroes
	Hire Heroes USA
	Workforce 1 Veterans Center
	U.S. Vets
	VetJobs.com
Job retention and mentoring	American Corporate Partners
	Workforce Opportunity Services

Overall, the unemployment rate for veterans is about 2 percentage points higher than for others—10 percent versus 8 percent in 2012. (The gap is wider among the young.) Many donors and charities are now focusing on closing that differential. For instance, since 2011, the U.S. Chamber of Commerce's Hiring our Heroes program has held more than 400 employment fairs for veterans and servicemembers, resulting in 14,100 job placements. Corporate philanthropies have been particularly effective in linking vets to jobs. Many companies are finding that hiring veterans can be good for the firm as well as for society, and especially useful for filling skilled positions that would otherwise lack adequate candidates. Training veterans, matching them to work openings, and mentoring them so they succeed are the main things philanthropists are concentrating on at present.

	Examples of donors
	Walmart, Ernst & Young, Martin Whitman, Richard Haydon, Steve Barnes, Ted Lachowicz
	Ewing Marion Kauffman Foundation
	Prudential, Merck, Johnson & Johnson
	FINRA Foundation
	Iraq-Afghanistan Deployment Impact Fund
	JPMorgan Chase
	Charles and Helen Schwab Foundation, Iraq-Afghanistan Deployment Impact Fund, Prudential, Walmart, JPMorgan Chase, California Wellness Foundation
	GE
	FedEx, Toyota
	Accenture, Boeing, TriWest
	Call of Duty Endowment, 7-Eleven, MedAssets, USO
	Robin Hood Foundation
	Home Depot, The Ahmanson Foundation
	Veterans of Foreign Wars
	Home Depot, JPMorgan Chase
	Prudential, Merck, Johnson & Johnson

 # Education

	Examples of service providers
Direct education expenses	Pat Tillman Foundation
	Army Emergency Relief (Scholarships for spouses and military children)
	Special Operations Warrior Foundation (Scholarships for military children)
	Student Veterans of America
Indirect education expenses	Student Veterans of America
	Pat Tillman Foundation
Academic support	Student Veterans of America
	Posse Foundation
	American Council on Education
Social support	Student Veterans of America
	Posse Foundation
	CUNY Project for Return and Opportunity in Veterans Education
	American Council on Education
	Peer Advisors for Veterans Education

There are charities that focus on educating the children of the fallen and other specialized groups, but thanks to today's rich G.I. Bill, college tuition is not an obstacle for most veterans. Staying on task until a degree is completed, however, is sometimes an issue. A typical veteran on campus today is 5–10 years older than the average college student. He or she often has a family. So making the social adjustment to college, getting appropriate mentoring from campus authorities, financing the interstitial periods between semesters, and staying in school and finishing a diploma are the toughest hurdles. Very recently, some smart donors, charities, and colleges have begun to understand and solve these issues.

	Examples of donors
	NFL, Guinness, Under Armour
	Armed Forces Relief Trust, Association of Military Banks of America, USAA Foundation, California Community Foundation, Jasam Foundation, Goldman Sachs Gives
	Birdies for the Brave Foundation
	Google, PNC Bank, Illinois Patriot Education Fund
	Google, Prudential, Call of Duty Endowment, Charles and Helen Schwab Foundation
	NFL, Guinness, Under Armour
	Google, Prudential, Call of Duty Endowment, Charles and Helen Schwab Foundation
	Infor, Boston Foundation, Google
	Walmart, S. S. Kresge Foundation
	Google, Prudential, Call of Duty Endowment, Charles and Helen Schwab Foundation
	Boston Foundation, Google
	Robin Hood Foundation
	Walmart, S. S. Kresge Foundation
	Bristol-Myers Squibb Foundation, McCormick Foundation, Major League Baseball, University of Michigan

Physical Health

	Examples of service providers
Amputations	Center for the Intrepid
Burns	Operation Mend
Genitourinary trauma	Operation Mend
Spinal injuries	Freedom Service Dogs of America
	Paralyzed Veterans of America
Blindness	Operation Mend
Hearing loss	
Polytrauma	Richard Roudebush V.A. Hospital, Indiana, Veterans Enhanced Services Initiative
Increasing access to care	Disabled American Veterans: V.A. transportation network
	V.A. mobile enrollment van
	Air Compassion for Veterans
	Operation Homefront
Adaptive sports	Disabled Sports USA
	Higher Ground Sun Valley
Military competence of health workers	Swords to Plowshares: competency training
	University of North Carolina: citizen soldier support program
Women's health	Swords to Plowshares

Some of today's most heartfelt private help for servicemembers and veterans is being offered to nurse the injured back to health. Philanthropists have found important niches where they can make crucial enhancements in the treatment provided by the government. The universe of severely injured individuals is limited—less than 15,000 of the 2.4 million Americans who were deployed to Iraq or Afghanistan were hurt seriously enough to be evacuated from the theater. Thus, dedicated philanthropic efforts can have noticeable and lasting effects. Listed below are examples of the range of services now being offered. Not all of these are strictly medical. Programs that help rehabilitate wounded vets by involving them in "adaptive sports" and outdoor activities like bike racing, mountain climbing, and fishing have proven popular with donors and veterans alike.

Examples of donors
Intrepid Fallen Heroes Fund, Iraq-Afghanistan Deployment Impact Fund
Katz Family Foundation, Iraq-Afghanistan Deployment Impact Fund
Katz Family Foundation, Iraq-Afghanistan Deployment Impact Fund
Anschutz Foundation, El Pomar Foundation
Alcoa Foundation, Wells Fargo
Katz Family Foundation, Iraq-Afghanistan Deployment Impact Fund
Lilly Endowment
Farmer Family Foundation
American Airlines
BAE Systems, Iraq-Afghanistan Deployment Impact Fund, JPMorgan Chase
Bob Woodruff Foundation
Sun Valley, Eddie Bauer
Charles and Helen Schwab Foundation, Iraq-Afghanistan Deployment Impact Fund, Prudential, Walmart, JPMorgan Chase, California Wellness Foundation
Duke Endowment, Red Sox Foundation
California Wellness Foundation

Mental Health

	Examples of service providers
Brain injury and traumatic stress	National Intrepid Center of Excellence and satellite centers
	Shepherd Center SHARE Military Initiative
	Bergin University of Canine Studies—Assistance Dog Institute
Substance abuse	Phoenix Multisport
	New Directions
Sexual trauma	Service Women's Action Network
Research	National Intrepid Center of Excellence and satellite centers
	RAND Corporation
Increasing access to care	Give an Hour
	NYU School of Medicine Military Family Clinic
	VetsPrevail
	Scott & White Military Mental Health Services
	Massachusetts General Hospital: Home Base program
Military competence of health workers	Massachusetts General Hospital: Home Base program
	Give an Hour
	Swords to Plowshares: competency training
	University of North Carolina: citizen soldier support program
	National Association of Social Workers—New York State Chapter
Reducing stigma	Advertising Council
	Got Your Six

Private counseling services outside the official clinics run by the Departments of Defense and Veterans Affairs are valued by veterans and members of the military because of the special privacy often desired for mental-health care. Also, family members of National Guard and Reserve and veterans are generally not covered at public clinics, though they can be stressed by overseas deployments and by combat injuries just as the servicemembers themselves are. So there are many opportunities for philanthropy to provide enlightened mental-health services, research, and support, which are likely to be priorities for charities and donors for some years to come.

Examples of donors
Intrepid Fallen Heroes Fund, Iraq-Afghanistan Deployment Impact Fund
Marcus Foundation
Harmon Recovery Foundation, Mike Altschuler Foundation, Triwest Healthcare Alliance
Iraq-Afghanistan Deployment Impact Fund
Intrepid Fallen Heroes Fund, Iraq-Afghanistan Deployment Impact Fund
Iraq-Afghanistan Deployment Impact Fund
Eli Lilly and Company Foundation, Robin Hood Foundation, Case Foundation, Bristol-Myers Squibb Foundation
Robin Hood Foundation
Goldman Sachs Gives, Pepsi Refresh, Robin Hood Foundation
Iraq-Afghanistan Deployment Impact Fund through the Dallas Foundation
McCormick Foundation, Major League Baseball
McCormick Foundation, Major League Baseball
Eli Lilly and Company Foundation, Case Foundation, Bristol-Myers Squibb Foundation
Charles and Helen Schwab Foundation, Iraq-Afghanistan Deployment Impact Fund, Prudential, Walmart, JPMorgan Chase, California Wellness Foundation
Duke Endowment, Red Sox Foundation
New York State Health Foundation
Iraq-Afghanistan Deployment Impact Fund
ABC, CBS, NBC Universal, HBO

Family and Community

	Examples of service providers
Family support	USO
	National Military Family Association
	Blue Star Families
	Our Military Kids
	National Math & Science Initiative: Initiative for Military Families
	Military Child Education Coalition
	Sesame Workshop
	Project Sanctuary
Bereavement services	Tragedy Assistance Program for Survivors (TAPS)
	Navy SEAL Foundation
Support for the severely wounded and/or their caregivers	Fisher House Foundation
	Special Operations Warrior Foundation
	Hero Miles
	Operation Homefront
	Our Military Kids
	Warrior and Family Support Center at SAMMC
	Red Cross resiliency training, Wounded Warrior Care
	Sentinels of Freedom
	Wounded Warrior Project
	Yellow Ribbon Fund
Community re-integration	Community Blueprint
	Easter Seals TriState
	Illinois Joining Forces
	Veterans Outreach Center
Connections with other veterans, and continuation of service	Iraq and Afghanistan Veterans of America
	American Legion
	Wounded Warrior Project
	Buddy to Buddy
	Team Red, White, and Blue
	Team Rubicon
	The Mission Continues

Community services of the sort that philanthropists have long supported can be very helpful to veterans and their families as they transition to civilian life. The possibilities for philanthropists here are wide: everything from programs that support caregivers to bereavement services, from efforts that enhance the education provided for military children to various fraternal organizations offering veterans personal support, sporting challenges, and social life.

Examples of donors
American Airlines, AT&T, Coca-Cola
BAE Systems, Bob Woodruff Foundation, Newman's Own, Fisher House Foundation, Iraq-Afghanistan Deployment Impact Fund
AG Foundation, BAE Systems, Newman's Own, United Concordia
Target, General Dynamics, Klarman Family Foundation
Lockheed Martin, BAE Systems, Northrop Grumman, Sarah and Ross Perot Jr. Foundation
HEB, BAE Systems, Serco, AT&T, Deloitte, Sid W. Richardson Foundation
Iraq-Afghanistan Deployment Impact Fund
Sam's Club
BAE Systems, DynCorp International, Fisher House Foundation, Prudential
Birdies for the Brave Foundation
Fisher House Foundation
Birdies for the Brave Foundation
Fisher House Foundation
BAE Systems, Iraq-Afghanistan Deployment Impact Fund, JPMorgan Chase
Target, General Dynamics, Klarman Family Foundation
Returning Heroes Home Foundation
Iraq-Afghanistan Deployment Impact Fund, Continental Airlines
American Airlines, Chevron, General Dynamics, AT&T
Raytheon, Call of Duty Endowment, USAA Foundation
JPMorgan Chase
Bristol Myers Squibb Foundation, ITT Exelis
Farmer Family Foundation, Carol Ann and Ralph Haile Jr./US Bank Foundation
McCormick Foundation, Tawani Foundation
New York State Health Foundation
Triad Foundation, Rosenthal Family Foundation, Prudential, Iraq-Afghanistan Deployment Impact Fund
USAA Foundation
Raytheon, Call of Duty Endowment, USAA Foundation
McCormick Foundation, Major League Baseball
Military Officers Association of America, K-Swiss
Google, Goldman Sachs Gives, Palantir, Home Depot
New Profit, Novo Nordisk, Paul E. Singer Foundation, Bob Woodruff Foundation

$ Legal / Financial / Housing

	Examples of service providers
Legal assistance	Connecticut Veterans Legal Center
	Legal Services NYC Veterans Justice Project
	John Marshall Law School Veterans Clinic
	New York State Unified Court System (Veterans Treatment Court)
	Swords to Plowshares
Financial planning and protection	VeteransPlus
	CredAbility
	Army Emergency Relief: personal financial management course
Emergency funds	Operation Homefront
	Air Force Aid Society
	Army Emergency Relief
	Coast Guard Mutual Assistance
	Navy-Marine Corps Relief Society
	PenFed Foundation
	USA Cares
Home ownership and adaptive housing	Military Warriors Support Foundation
	Volunteers of America
	Operation Homefront
	Building Homes for Heroes
	Habitat for Humanity
Homelessness	Veterans Village of San Diego
	Swords to Plowshares
	U.S. Vets
	Jericho Project
	Doe Fund
	Pathways to Housing

Though veterans are, on the whole, less prone to poverty than other Americans, some inevitably face financial troubles. Eliminating debt, finding housing, and solving legal problems are all places where philanthropy can help. Aid ranging from free financial counseling to pro bono *lawyering to help with home modification is now on offer through various charitable efforts. There are many openings for more such efforts in communities across the country.*

Examples of donors
Community Foundation for Greater New Haven, Udell Family Fund
Robin Hood Foundation
Tawani Foundation
New York State Health Foundation
Charles and Helen Schwab Foundation, Iraq-Afghanistan Deployment Impact Fund, Prudential, Walmart, JPMorgan Chase, California Wellness Foundation
Citigroup, Ryder, Wells Fargo
Citigroup
Armed Forces Relief Trust, Association of Military Banks of America, USAA Foundation, California Community Foundation, Jasam Foundation, Goldman Sachs Gives
BAE Systems, Iraq-Afghanistan Deployment Impact Fund, JPMorgan Chase
USAA Foundation, General Dynamics, California Community Trust
Armed Forces Relief Trust, Association of Military Banks of America, USAA Foundation, California Community Foundation, Jasam Foundation, Goldman Sachs Gives
USAA Foundation, Boston Foundation, California Community Foundation
USAA Foundation, TriWest, Karakin Foundation
Pentagon Federal Credit Union
Remington Partners, Fannie Mae, Iraq-Afghanistan Deployment Impact Fund
Home Depot, JPMorgan Chase
Home Depot
Iraq-Afghanistan Deployment Impact Fund, Bank of America, Wells Fargo
JPMorgan Chase
Home Depot, Lowe's, Dow Chemical, Citigroup
Home Depot, Iraq-Afghanistan Deployment Impact Fund
Charles and Helen Schwab Foundation, Iraq-Afghanistan Deployment Impact Fund, Prudential, Walmart, JPMorgan Chase, California Wellness Foundation
Home Depot, The Ahmanson Foundation
Robin Hood Foundation
Robin Hood Foundation
William S. Abell Foundation

WHAT THE
FEDERAL
GOVERNMENT
PROVIDES

While not exhaustive, this list outlines the major services provided by the government to servicemembers, veterans, and their dependents.

For ease of comparison, the list's pages are set up to mirror the previous list: **What Donors and Charities are Doing**. Both lists are organized by the same topics at the top of each page, and the same need categories down the left side of the page. That will allow you to quickly compare the existing private and public footprints in every area as you plan your own philanthropy.

 **Employment**

Need	During service commitment	
	Servicemember	Dependents
Training and certification	Internship program for wounded, ill, injured servicemembers recovering at military medical facilities (DoD Operation Warfighter)	Assistance with interstate professional licensure transfer for military spouses (Joining Forces, USA 4 Military Families)
		Financial support for spouses seeking professional certification (DoD My CAA)
Placement	Jobs database and hiring events specifically for members of reserve components (DoD Hero2Hired)	Recruitment and employment program for military spouses (DoD MSEP)
Job retention and mentoring	National committee protecting reservist employment (DoD ESGR)	
	Prohibition of employment discrimination based on military service (USERRA)	

After service commitment	
Veteran	**Dependents**
Transfer of military to civilian professional license (Joining Forces, USA 4 Military Families)	
Individualized rehab, training, program for service-disabled veterans (V.A. VR&E, VetSuccess)	
12 months of vocational training for veterans ages 35 to 60 (V.A. VRAP)	
Out-processing seminar helping servicemembers with employment resources (TAP/TransitionGPS)	
Tax credits for firms hiring veterans (VOW Act)	
Six months of intensive employment services at One-Stop Career Centers (DoL Gold Card)	
Online jobs databases with veterans focus (NRD Veterans Job Bank, DoL My Next Move)	
Feds Hire Vets program	
Public-private initiative to train and hire 100,000 veterans and military spouses (Joining Forces)	

 **Education**

Need	During service commitment	
	Servicemember	Dependents
Direct education expenses	Military academy, college, graduate school, training, or service-relevant civilian schooling	Limited financial assistance for spouses pursuing licensures or certifications (DoD MyCAA)
Indirect education expenses		
Academic support		Transfer academic credit for dependents moving between states with different schooling requirements. (Joining Forces, USA 4 Military Families)
Social support		

After service commitment	
Veteran	**Dependents**
Educational benefits up to cost of most expensive public university in state of residence (V.A. 9/11, Montgomery G.I. Bill, Reserve Educational Assistance Program)	Transfer of educational benefits from servicemember to dependents or survivors (V.A. TEB)
Financial assistance to make up difference between G.I. Bill funding and cost of private university (V.A. Yellow Ribbon Program)	
Transfer military training and skills to academic credit (Joining Forces, USA 4 Military Families)	
Academic skills course in preparation for post-secondary education (Veterans Upward Bound)	

Physical Health

Need	During service commitment	
	Servicemember	Dependents[1]
Amputations	Integrated prosthetic and physical rehab programs (DoD Center for the Intrepid, DoD Military Advanced Training Center)	
Burns	DoD San Antonio Military Medical Center Burn Unit	
Genitourinary trauma	Reconstructive surgery and some fertility treatments	
Spinal injuries	DoD research and treatment centers for spinal-cord injuries (Spinal Cord Injury Research Program)	
Blindness	Over 180 research and treatment centers for vision problems (DoD Vision Center of Excellence)	
Hearing loss	Research and coordinating center for auditory health (DoD Hearing Center of Excellence)	
Polytrauma	Four inpatient and 21 other sites for long-term care (V.A. Polytrauma System of Care)	
Increasing access to care	Full-service healthcare system combining military and civilian providers (DoD MHS and Tricare)	
Adaptive sports	V.A. Adaptive Sports Program	
Military competence of health workers		
Women's health		

1. Family of active-duty servicemembers are eligible for these trauma services, but rarely require them.

After service commitment	
Veteran	**Dependents**
Integrated prosthetic and physical rehab programs (DoD Center for the Intrepid, DoD Military Advanced Training Center)	
DoD San Antonio Military Medical Center Burn Unit	
Reconstructive surgery and some fertility treatments	
24 regional centers and 134 primary-care teams provide long-term care and access to benefits through (V.A. Spinal Cord Injury and Disorder Centers)	
Over 180 research and treatment centers for vision problems (DoD Vision Center of Excellence)	
Research and coordinating center for auditory health (DoD Hearing Center of Excellence)	
4 inpatient and 21 other sites for long-term care (V.A. Polytrauma System of Care)	
MHS and Tricare (for military retirees and dependents only)	
Veterans healthcare system with 152 hospitals and 1,400 community-based clinics (V.A. VHA)	
V.A. Rural Transportation Program and 230 emergency shuttle vehicles	
V.A. Adaptive Sports Program	
Specialty care, facilities, and health-provider training for health issues facing women vets	

Mental Health

Need	During service commitment	
	Servicemember	Dependents
Brain injury and traumatic stress	Seven clinical treatment centers for psychological health and brain injury, DoD National Intrepid Center of Excellence (NICoE) and satellite centers	
	Clinical treatment through DoD MHS and Tricare	
Substance abuse		
Sexual trauma	Intensive residential treatment (V.A. Women's Trauma Recovery Program)	
Research	Three centers that research, develop, and disseminate technology for psychological health and brain-injury treatment (DoD Defense Center of Excellence)	
	Research center for psychological health and brain injury DoD National Intrepid Center of Excellence (NICoE)	
Increasing access to care	Coaching to help find new providers when a duty station changes (DoD inTransition)	
Military competence of health workers		
Reducing stigma	Program incorporating mental-health screening and referral into primary care (DoD RESPECT-Mil)	

After service commitment	
Veteran	**Dependents**
DoD MHS and Tricare (retirees only)	
Veterans' healthcare system with 152 centers and 1,400 community-based outpatient clinics (V.A. VHA, Office of Mental Health Operations)	
Substance-abuse treatment programs at most V.A. facilities (V.A. SUD)	
Intensive residential treatment (V.A. Women's Trauma Recovery Program)	
Seven centers for research and education about PTSD (V.A. National Center for PTSD)	
70 vehicles provide counselors, counseling space, and communication centers to veterans far from facilities (V.A. Mobile Vet Centers)	
Readjustment Counseling Service PTSD training for primary-healthcare providers in MHS	

Family and Community

Need	During service commitment
	Servicemember
Deployment support	Recreation and leisure programs and resources at most military installations (DoD Morale, Welfare, and Recreation)
Post-deployment Family Reintegration	DoD Morale, Welfare, and Recreation
	Support services for reserve component families (DoD Yellow Ribbon Reintegration Program)
Bereavement services	
Support for the severely wounded and/ or their caregivers	Units support comprehensive healing process for servicemembers requiring more than six months of care (DoD Warrior Transition Units)
Community reintegration	Guidance and coordination for community efforts (DoD Joint Chiefs of Staff Office of Warrior and Family Support)
Connection with other veterans	

		After service commitment	
	Dependents	Veteran	Dependents
	Support services for reserve component families (DoD Yellow Ribbon Reintegration Program)		
	Unit-based support groups usually led by commanding officer's spouse (DoD Family Readiness Groups)		
	Resources for families with special needs (DoD Exceptional Family Member Program)		
	Initiative to increase access to child care for military children (Joining Forces, USA 4 Military Families)		
	50 support and resource centers for wounded servicemembers and their families recovering and transitioning out of military (DoD Soldier and Family Assistance Centers)	V.A. Long Term Care	V.A. Extended Caregiver Support Services
			V.A. Caregiver Support Coordinators

$ Legal / Financial / Housing

Need	During service commitment	
	Servicemember	**Dependents**
Legal assistance	Ensuring child-custody cases are not determined by parental deployments (Joining Forces, USA 4 Military Families)	
	Help with legal affairs before mobilization or deployment—for instance, guidance on family, civil, financial, or immigration law (DoD Legal Assistance Program, Joining Forces)	
Access to benefits		
	Centralized portal for managing benefits throughout military and veteran life (eBenefits)	
Financial planning and protection	Office to protect servicemembers, veterans, and families from predatory financial practices (U.S. Treasury Consumer Financial Protection Bureau Office of Servicemember Affairs)	
Financial compensation and insurance	One-time payout for servicemembers who suffer traumatic injuries (V.A. TSGLI)	Low-cost life insurance for families of servicemembers (V.A. FSGLI)
	Low-cost life insurance (V.A. SGLI)	
Home ownership and adaptive housing	Protection against foreclosure during deployments (Servicemembers' Civil Relief Act)	
Homelessness	Military housing or housing allowance	

After service commitment	
Veteran	**Dependents**
Legal assistance for retirees	
Diversionary courts that consider military history in ruling on criminal cases (Joining Forces, USA 4 Military Families, Veteran Treatment Courts)	
Out-processing seminar to connect servicemembers with benefits (TAP/Transition GPS)	
Grants to nonprofit organizations to help homeless vets and their families connect with benefits and case management (V.A. SSVF)	
Personal financial planning services (V.A. SSVF)	
Monthly cash transfer based on age and/or disabilities received as a result of military service (V.A. Disability Compensation, V.A. Pension)	Monthly payment to surviving dependents of deceased servicemembers or veterans to replace lost income (DoD Survivor Benefits Plan, V.A. Death Pension, V.A. Dependency and Indemnity Compensation)
Post-separation life insurance (V.A. VGLI)	
Mortgage loan guarantee (V.A. Home Loan)	V.A. Survivor Home Loan
Grant to build or renovate housing for those with service-connected disabilities (V.A. Specially Adapted Housing Program)	
Housing counseling services (V.A. SSVF)	
10,000 housing vouchers for homeless vets, families per year (HUD-VASH)	
17 homeless veterans services hubs open 24/7 (V.A. Community Resource and Referral Center)	
300 centers to provide readjustment counseling and referral services (V.A. Vet Centers)	

RAPID
EXPANSION
OF THE
DEPARTMENT
OF VETERANS
AFFAIRS

Over the last decade, there has been an enormous infusion of government spending and public employment on behalf of former and current members of the military. The Department of Veterans Affairs has been one of the fastest-expanding parts of the federal government, with its total employment rising 45 percent over the last decade and its total spending jumping to three times its previous level.

Department of Veterans Affairs Budget and Full-time Employees

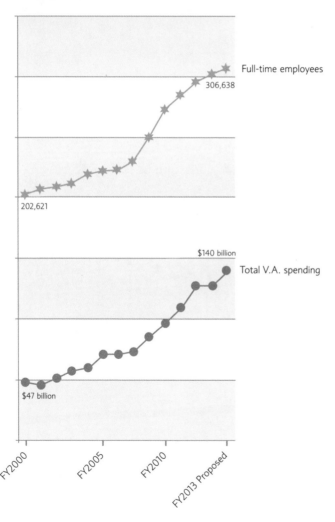

Full-time employees

306,638

202,621

$140 billion

Total V.A. spending

$47 billion

FY2000   FY2005   FY2010   FY2013 Proposed

Growth of Health Payments

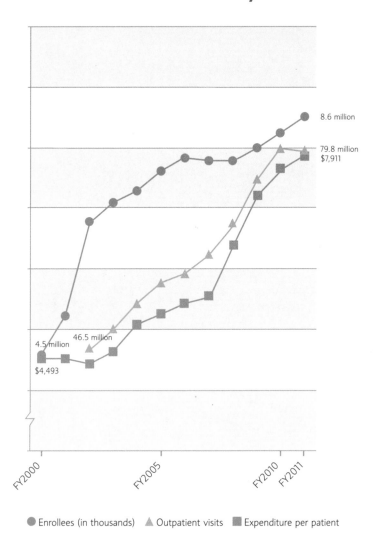

8.6 million

79.8 million
$7,911

4.5 million

46.5 million

$4,493

FY2000   FY2005   FY2010   FY2011

● Enrollees (in thousands)   ▲ Outpatient visits   ■ Expenditure per patient

Growth of Benefit Payments

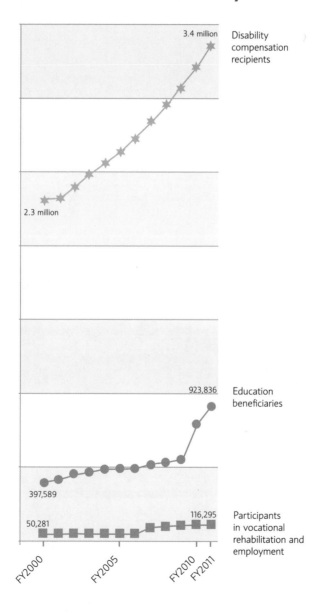

3.4 million — Disability compensation recipients

2.3 million

923,836 — Education beneficiaries

397,589

50,281

116,295 — Participants in vocational rehabilitation and employment

FY2000   FY2005   FY2010 FY2011

Rise in Disability Recipients by Rated Percentage of Disablement

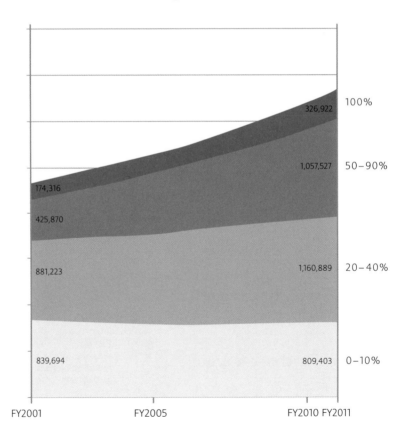

Overall Resources of the Department of Veterans Affairs

Budget FY2012	$126,949,000,000
Veterans Health Administration	$53,378,000,000
Long-term care	$6,671,000,000
Mental-health care	$5,800,000,000
Iraq/Afghanistan program	$2,769,000,000
Prosthetics	$2,330,000,000
Spinal-cord injury	$547,000,000
Traumatic brain injury	$201,000,000
Telehome health	$316,000,000
Women-specific medical care	$343,000,000
Medical Research	$581,000,000
Veterans Benefit Administration	$67,740,000,000
Compensation and pensions	$51,238,000,000
Readjustment benefits[1]	$12,108,000,000
Insurance	$100,000,000
Housing	$1,659,000,000
National Cemeteries Administration	$251,000,000
Infrastructure	
Hospitals	152
Community-based outpatient clinics	817
Vet centers	300
Regional benefits offices	56
Community resource and referral centers	17
National cemeteries	131
Personnel	
Medical care employees	259,329
Benefits employees	20,646
Compensation and pensions	15,862
Education	2,030
Vocational rehabilitation	1,443

1. Includes education

INDEX

ABOUT THE PHILANTHROPY ROUNDTABLE

The Philanthropy Roundtable is America's leading network of charitable donors working to strengthen our free society, uphold donor intent, and protect the freedom to give. Our members include individual philanthropists, families, and private foundations.

Mission

The Philanthropy Roundtable's mission is to foster excellence in philanthropy, to protect philanthropic freedom, to assist donors in achieving their philanthropic intent, and to help donors advance liberty, opportunity, and personal responsibility in America and abroad.

Principles
- Philanthropic freedom is essential to a free society.
- A vibrant private sector generates the wealth that makes philanthropy possible.
- Voluntary private action offers solutions for many of society's most pressing challenges.
- Excellence in philanthropy is measured by results, not by good intentions.
- A respect for donor intent is essential for philanthropic integrity.

Services

World-Class Conferences
The Philanthropy Roundtable connects you with other savvy donors. Held across the nation throughout the year, our meetings assemble grantmakers and experts to develop strategies and solutions for local, state, and national giving. You will hear from innovators in K–12 education, economic opportunity, higher education, national security, and other fields. Our Annual Meeting is the Roundtable's flagship event, gathering the nation's most public-spirited and influential philanthropists for debates, how-to sessions, and discussions on the best ways for private individuals to achieve powerful results through their giving. The Annual Meeting is a stimulating and enjoyable way to meet principled donors seeking the breakthroughs that can solve our nation's greatest challenges.

Breakthrough Groups
Our Breakthrough Groups—focused program areas—build a critical mass of donors around a topic where dramatic results are within reach. Breakthrough Groups become a springboard to help donors achieve lasting results with their philanthropy. Our specialized staff assist grantmakers committed to making careful investments. The Roundtable's K–12 education program is our largest and longest-running Breakthrough Group. This network helps donors zero in on the most promising school reforms. We are the industry-leading convener for philanthropists seeking systemic improvements through competition and parental choice, administrative freedom and accountability, student-centered technology, enhanced teaching and school leadership, and high standards and expectations for students of all backgrounds. We foster productive collaboration among donors of varied ideological perspectives who are united by a devotion to educational excellence.

A Powerful Voice

The Roundtable's public policy project, the Alliance for Charitable Reform (ACR), works to advance the principles and preserve the rights of private giving. ACR educates legislators and policymakers about the central role of charitable giving in American life and the crucial importance of protecting philanthropic freedom—the ability of individuals and private organizations to determine how and where to direct their charitable assets. Active in Washington, D.C., and in the states, ACR protects charitable giving, defends the diversity of charitable causes, and battles intrusive government regulation. We believe that our nation's capacity for private initiative to address problems must not be burdened with costly or crippling constraints.

Protection of Donor Interests

The Philanthropy Roundtable is the leading force in American philanthropy to protect donor intent. Generous givers want assurance that their money will be used for the specific charitable aims and purposes they believe in, not redirected to some other agenda. Unfortunately, donor intent is usually violated in increments, as foundation staff and trustees neglect or misconstrue the founder's values and drift into other purposes. Through education, practical guidance, legislative action, and individual consultation, The Philanthropy Roundtable is active in guarding donor intent. We are happy to advise you on steps you can take to ensure that your mission and goals are protected.

Must-read Publications

Philanthropy, the Roundtable's quarterly magazine, is packed with beautifully written real-life stories. It offers practical examples, inspiration, detailed information, history, and clear guidance on the differences between giving that is great and giving that disappoints. We also publish a series of guidebooks which provide detailed information on the very best ways to be effective in particular aspects of philanthropy. These guidebooks are compact, brisk, and readable. Most focus on one particular area of giving—for instance, Catholic schools, support for veterans, anti-poverty programs, environmental projects, and technology in education. Real-life examples, hard numbers, management experiences of other donors, recent history, and policy guidance are presented to inform and inspire savvy donors.

Join the Roundtable Today

When working with The Philanthropy Roundtable, members are better equipped to achieve long-lasting success with their charitable giving. Your membership with the Roundtable will make you part of a potent network that understands philanthropy and strengthens our free society. Philanthropy Roundtable members range from *Forbes* 400 individuals and the largest American foundations to small family foundations and donors just beginning their charitable careers. Our members include:

- Individuals and families
- Private foundations
- Community foundations
- Eligible donor advisors
- Corporate giving programs
- Charities which devote more than half of their budget to external grants

Philanthropists who contribute at least $50,000 annually to charitable causes are eligible to become members and register for most Roundtable programs. Roundtable events provide you with a solicitation-free environment.

For more information on The Philanthropy Roundtable or to learn about our individual program areas, please call (202) 822-8333 or email main@ PhilanthropyRoundtable.org.

ABOUT THE AUTHOR

Thomas Meyer is the program manager for veterans and military-family services at The Philanthropy Roundtable. He graduated with distinction in sociology from Yale University before completing a Fox Fellowship at the University of Cambridge. While there, his research and fieldwork with the U.S. and U.K. armies focused on understanding how junior military officers adapted to counterinsurgency operations in Iraq and Afghanistan. His writing on the topic appears in *Security Studies*. Before he began researching the military, he grew up in an Army family, moving nine times across six countries. He currently lives in Washington, D.C.